Arkansas Geography

The Physical Landscape and the Historical-Cultural Setting

HUBERT B. STROUD
GERALD T. HANSON

ROSE PUBLISHING COMPANY
Little Rock, Arkansas

PREFACE

This text on the geography of Arkansas examines the relationships between man and his surroundings. The hydrologic (water) cycle is used as a framework for studying the various parts of the physical environment of Arkansas. These chapters set the stage for a consideration of Arkansas' natural regions, early settlement, population change and other important human activities that give Arkansas its character.

Although numerous publications are available on specific Arkansas topics including climate, water resources, population change, and forest statistics, none addresses both the physical and cultural geography of Arkansas and none provides a comprehensive view of our state in a single volume. This text fills this void by providing an up-to-date book on Arkansas' physical, historical and cultural settings.

Maps are used as a primary illustrative tool in this text. Some of the maps are original; others are updated revisions or generalizations of existing maps. Few if any of these maps have appeared previously in published form.

The authors would like to acknowledge the assistance of Loyal A. Quandt, Soil Conservation Service; Wendel Adams, Department of Economic Development; officials at the National Weather Service; James Tiner and Randall Leister, Arkansas Forestry Commission; officials at the Arkansas Geological Commission; Randal Young, Division of Soil and Water Resources, Arkansas Soil and Water Conservation Service; and officials at the Water Resources Division of the United States Geological Survey for their assistance during the early stages of the research for this text. A special note of thanks is extended to Tom Foti who stimulated interest in Arkansas by his work on the natural divisions of the state. Finally, appreciation is extended to Walter Nunn for his editorial suggestions and to our wives for their suggestions, encouragement and patience during the preparation of this manuscript.

May 16, 1981

Gerald Hanson
Hubert Stroud

CONTENTS

PART ONE — PHYSICAL GEOGRAPHY

PART TWO — CULTURAL GEOGRAPHY

LIST OF FIGURES

LIST OF TABLES

PART ONE
PHYSICAL GEOGRAPHY

Chapter I

INTRODUCTION

Purpose

This book on the geography of Arkansas is intended to help you better understand the nature of geography and at the same time better understand your state.

The book will explain the differences we see in Arkansas' land from the mountains in the north and west to the flat land in the eastern part of the state. We will examine settlement patterns and develop an understanding of Arkansas' cultural landscape. We will study several important geographical concepts important to Arkansas and other states and countries.

Finally, this book will show you how understanding the geography of Arkansas will help you to better use our land and resources. This study of the geography of Arkansas will improve your understanding of the location, relative amount, and quality of the state's rich farmland, extensive forests, vast water resources, and several other important features. This will help you use the resources and land wisely and conserve them for the future.

Geography: Its Scope and Nature

The word **geography** comes from a Greek word which means "description of the earth." Modern geography has expanded and is concerned with man and the earth, and explanation as well as description.

Geographers are concerned with three kinds of concepts: (1) the location of mankind over the earth and its influence on the use of the earth; (2) the relationships between man and the physical environment; and (3) the regional framework and the study of specific regions.

Geography is concerned with the concept of **location** and the explanation of these locations. A geographer first determines where something is located on the surface of the earth. He then looks for groupings or concentrations of the items or elements being mapped. Finally, the geographer undertakes the sometimes difficult task of explaining the groupings or concentrations that have been established. For example, the geographer might plot the location of Arkansas' population and then explain why relatively large numbers of people are living in Pulaski, Jefferson, and Washington counties while only a few people live in the mountainous regions of the Ozarks.

Geography looks at both the **natural landscape** and the man-made or **cultural landscape.** The natural landscape includes the air, weather, soils, plants, rocks, and water. These parts of the natural landscape are called the physical elements or natural environment. Later in the book, we will study how the weather is different for the various parts of our state.

For example, why do the Ouachita Mountains and the central and southern parts of the state get more rainfall than the northern sections? You will also look at the different kinds of soils and plants found in Arkansas. These are also part of the natural landscape. In addition to these physical elements we will look at the different landforms such as mountains and valleys in the state. These landforms make up part of the natural landscape which we see around us.

Geography also involves the cultural or manmade landscape, which may be defined as the structures added to the physical environment by the activities of man. Man thereby changes the natural landscape into the cultural landscape. He builds structures such as houses and barns or even entire communities or towns which greatly change the appearance of the landscape. Man also alters the landscape by farms, highways, dams and other structures. We will examine the different cultural landscapes in

Arkansas and discover why they are different. Is the cultural landscape around Little Rock the same as around Texarkana? How does a cotton farm landscape differ from a poultry farm in northwest Arkansas?

Concepts in Geography

Geography has many important ideas which help us to understand the landscape around us. Some of these ideas are **location, region, distribution, migration, change, culture,** and **scale.** We use these ideas each day when we go to school or back to our homes and in our travels in the state. **Location** is one of the most important ideas in geography.

For example, we all live in different houses which are at different places. One way to compare differences between places is to compare their locations. Look at Figure 1 and note the different towns. Each is at a different location. Which city is not on a railroad? Which city is on the biggest river? Which city has the largest area? By talking about location, we really are learning about differences in the **geography of our area.**

Region is another idea (concept) in geography. Regions are areas with limits or boundaries. For example, the state of Arkansas is a region because it has limits or boundaries. We call the state a political region. There are 50 political regions or states in the United States of America.

There are also many different kinds of regions is Arkansas. Each county in the state is a special type of political region. Our towns are also regions since they have boundaries. Look at Figure 2 and find the county in which you live.

We might also look at another kind of region. Eastern Arkansas has several farming regions. A rice-producing region is found around Stuttgart in Arkansas County and in several counties south

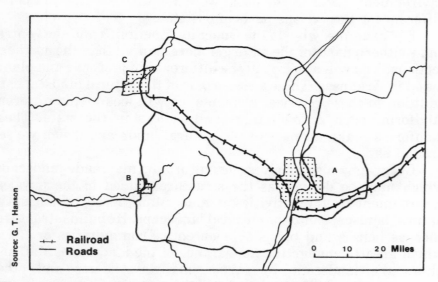

Figure 1. A Location Map showing three cities.

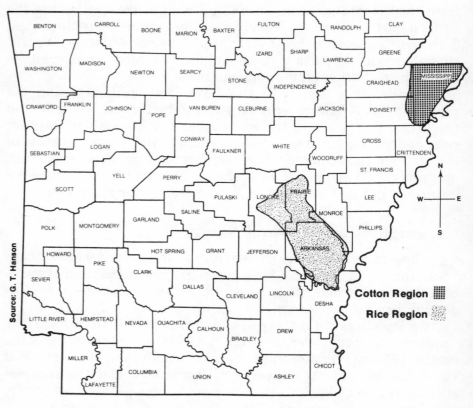

Figure 2. Regions in Arkansas.

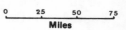

of Jonesboro. There are also cotton and soybean regions in eastern Arkansas (Figure 2). How can we tell the differences between regions? Remember in geography we are concerned about differences between places. Each region has one or more features which make it easy to identify. What would be the important feature of the rice-producing region in Figure 2?

One purpose of geography is to understand what different places are like. We can do this by looking at the geographic **distributions**. This is another idea we want to consider. One way to understand distribution is to look at the number of items found in an area. This is called density. How many towns are found in Figure 1? Count the number of classmates in your room. What is the density of the classroom? Geographic distribution also has a pattern to it. For example, we can find how many towns in Arkansas are along rivers. Since a river flows in a line-like pattern, we can say these towns have a linear pattern. If the towns were in a circle, then the pattern would be circular.

Movement of people and goods is another part of geography. How do people and goods get from one place to another? They are carried there by different means of transportation. They can go by car, bus, train, or plane. This movement is called **migration** and is a key idea in geography. Movement of people and goods is very important to understand. This illustrates one way in which our landscapes change. Consider how different Arkansas' landscape would look today if there had not been any migrations to our state. Or even more importantly, what if no new ideas or products entered our state? Later in this book we will look at many different migrations to Arkansas.

Change is a fifth geographic idea. Change is always occurring in our environment. Nothing remains the same in our landscape. From summer to winter our landscape changes as the leaves fall and the plants stop growing. Our towns and farms also change. New buildings replace old ones. Roads are built and houses are constructed as new people move into an area. In learning about Arkansas, we want to understand what changes occur and why they happen. Can you list the changes which have taken place in your town since you started going to school? Which changes have been the easiest to see?

Change and **culture** (our way of life) are closely related. Our ways of living change over time. In this book on Arkansas, we will learn about those changes. As our ways of living change, the landscape also changes.

Maps

A globe is the only true representation of the earth's surface. The earth is roughly spherical in shape and so is a globe. The globe portrays true distance, direction, shape, and area and provides a precise location for all points or places on the globe without distortion or error. The distance between continents or between cities (between New York City and London, for example) is accurately portrayed on globes. The shape of continents and all other objects on a globe are presented without distortion. Also distortion-free is the proper size (area) of the continents. Direction is also portrayed without misrepresentation.

With all these advantages of the globe, why would a geographer use maps? Globes have numerous disadvantages as well as the previously described advantages. Globes are expensive, difficult to store and only one side of the globe can be viewed at a time. Most importantly, they do not portray the detail that geographers need.

Suppose, for example, you as a student of the earth are interested in the layout of the streets in the city of Little Rock. Suppose further that you wanted to find the location of the Federal Building or the Capitol Mall in Little Rock. Imagine how large the globe would need to be if it were large enough to provide enough detail to find specific places in a city such as Little Rock. The globe would probably be larger than your school building, cost thousands of dollars, and require elevators, steps, or a ladder to enable you to climb around on this enormous sphere in an attempt to find Arkansas and then the city of Little Rock and its street pattern.

Because of the absence of detail on normal sized globes, maps which are simply take-offs from the globe are drawn to provide the detail that geographers and other people who are interested in finding the location of places on the earth need. Maps are also useful because geographers can plot all kinds of information on them. The location of rice production in Arkansas or the location of cities and towns in Arkansas, the United States, or for the entire world, are examples.

Maps are also useful because certain map projections portray the entire world on a single sheet of paper. This allows the geographer to compare the distribution of all kinds of information for the entire world on one page. A world map showing the location of the world's population (a population distribution map) is most useful and basic in geographic studies. These and many other types of maps are essential to the geographer and are used constantly even though the globe is the only accurate representation of the earth. Some distortion is inevitable in going from a sphere (the globe) to a flat map, but the geographer is willing to sacrifice the accuracy of some of the properties (area, shape, distance, or direction) in order to have a flat map that can be used in a number of important ways.

We use maps for special purposes. They show us how many people live in an area or what kinds of agriculture goes on there. Maps also can tell us what forms of transportation are found in an area. Location of towns, rivers, and other features can also be found on maps. By comparing maps of different places we are learning about the geography of a region. This is why there are so many maps in this book.

Maps may also be used to show the distribution of a particular feature or phenomenon at varying scales. In other words, a geographer studying rice production in Arkansas might first wish to show areas of rice production for the entire world to provide a broad perspective concerning the location and extent of rice production world-wide (Figure 3). The geographer might then provide a map of rice production in the United States to show where rice is grown in our nation and the extensiveness of this production (Figure 4). These two maps could be followed by a map of rice production in Arkansas. This map would provide a much more detailed look at where rice is grown in Arkansas and the variation in acreage by county in the state (Figure 5). As is obvious from this series of maps, rice production is strongly concentrated and limited to a few locations.

The world-wide view shows strong concentrations in parts of Asia, especially in northeast India, Southeast Asia, eastern China, and southern Japan. At the U. S. scale, it is obvious that rice production is limited to three locations—California's Central Valley, the coast of southeastern Texas and southwestern

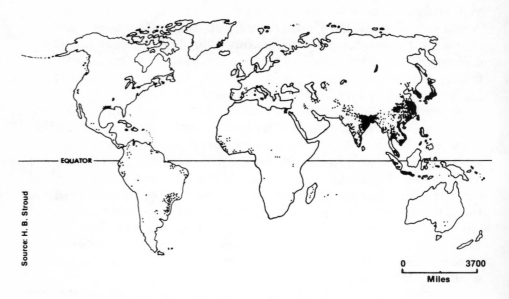

Source: H. B. Stroud

EQUATOR

0   3700
Miles

Figure 3. Rice production in the world.

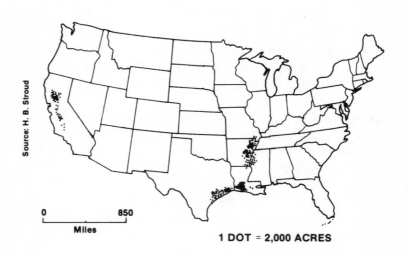

Source: H. B. Stroud

0   850
Miles

1 DOT = 2,000 ACRES

Figure 4. Rice production in the United States.

Louisiana, and eastern Arkansas.

The Arkansas map also shows the concentration of rice in eastern Arkansas and the two areas of eastern Arkansas where most of the rice is grown—in several counties from just south of Jonesboro to Brinkley and in the Grand Prairie around Stuttgart. These three maps illustrate a useful approach in geographic studies where the broad world-wide view is presented as a frame of reference for a study of rice production in Arkansas.

An indispensable kind of map in considering an area's terrain is the **topographic map**. Topographic maps represent, by the use of symbols, many important physical and cultural elements of an area. The terrain or topography of an area is portrayed by **contour lines**, lines connecting points of equal elevation above sea level.

Contour lines are drawn in brown and where terrain is rugged or steeply sloping the contours will be closely spaced. Flat land or gently sloping terrain has widely spaced contours.

These differences in the spacing of the contours are obvious on Figure 6, a topographic map of the hilly terrain along the foothills of the Ozarks and the flatland of the coastal plain. Figure 7 illustrates the relationship between irregularities of the surface (surface profile) and the spacing of contours. Hills or mountain tops are identified by contours that close on themselves until the highest point of the mountain or hill is reached.

Valleys are portrayed in the same manner except for the fact that **hachured contours** are used to indicate a depression or a valley. Hachures are short lines drawn on a map to represent differences in the slope of the ground. Hachured contours are used to distinguish valleys from hills and mountains and are the short lines drawn perpendicular to contour lines to illustrate a valley or depression. Hachured contours are used in Figure 7 to identify the valley in the illustration. Why do we need topographic maps? How are they useful to us? How are they useful to builders, to planners, to farmers, and to hikers?

The following rules regarding contour lines should help in understanding their usefulness:

1. Contour lines do not end. They will always be closed lines, although they may run off a particular map before doing so.
2. Contour lines never divide or intersect.
3. Contour lines are closer together on steep slopes than they are on gentle slopes.
4. Contour lines bend upstream into a "V" when crossing streams. They bend in the direction of downslope when crossing ridges.
5. Land on the inside of a closed contour line is higher, unless it is a hachured contour, indicating a depression (valley).

There are several parts to each map. All maps should have a **scale, direction symbols**, a **legend**, and **title**. The scale of a map can be given several ways. We will use the bar scale in the maps in the book. The bar scales are found at the bottom of the map. They tell us distance on the map.

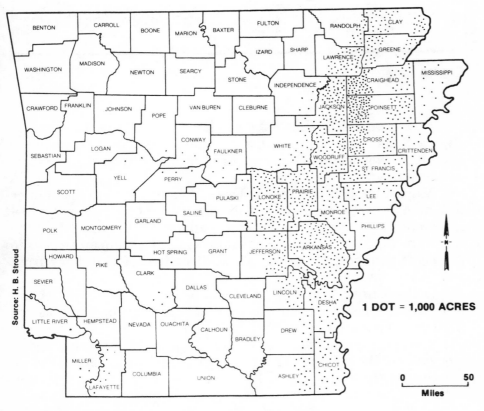

Source: H. B. Stroud

1 DOT = 1,000 ACRES

0   50
Miles

Figure 5. Rice production in Arkansas - 1978.

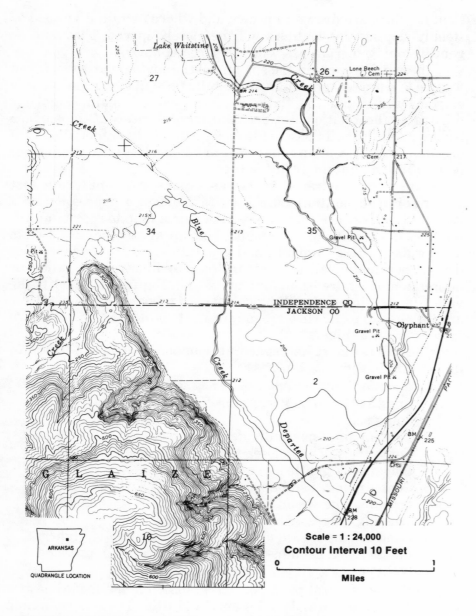

Figure 6. Topographic Map, Olyphant, Arkansas.

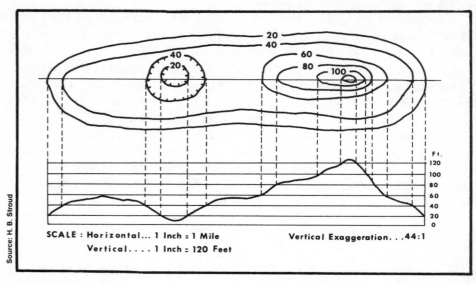

Source: H. B. Stroud

SCALE : Horizontal... 1 Inch = 1 Mile
Vertical.... 1 Inch = 120 Feet

Vertical Exaggeration...44:1

Figure 7.

How far is it from Little Rock to Texarkana? To find out, look at Figure 8 and measure in a straight line the distance between the two cities. Now compare the distance in inches with the bar scale distance.

Maps also show direction. We know that there are four major directions—north, south, east, and west. A compass rose or symbol is included on maps to show these directions. North is usually at the top of the map. This means that south is at the bottom and east is to the right and west to the left. What direction is Little Rock from your home town?

A third important part of the map is the legend. The legend tells the symbols used on the map. There may be symbols for highways, rivers, cities, or any other item. The title, the fourth part of a map, states what the map shows. If the map were showing the tree types of the state, it might be called **Trees of Arkansas.** Before we go into the next part of the book look at the key words and activities for this chapter.

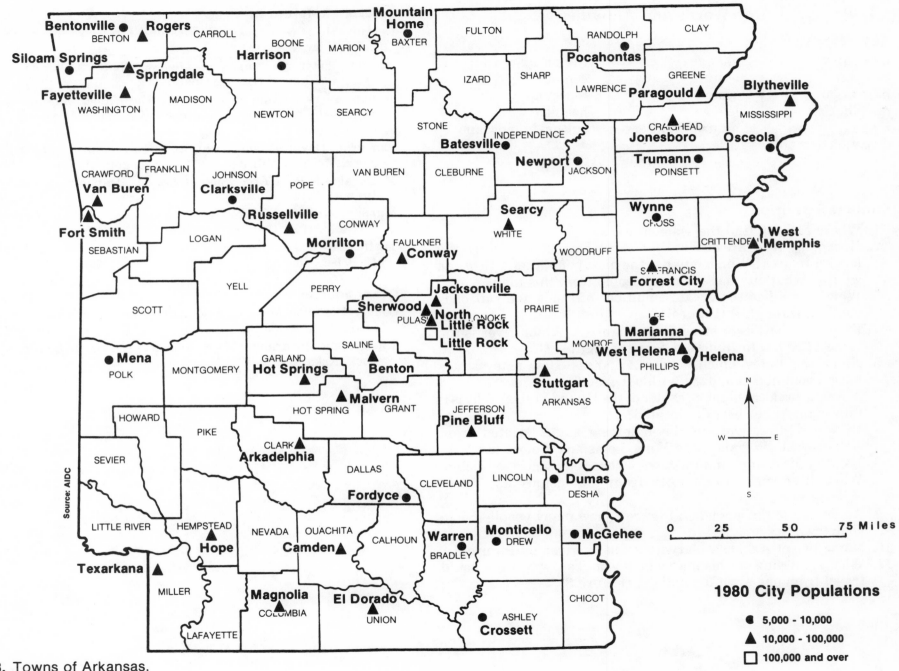

Figure 8. Towns of Arkansas.

Key Words and Activities

Key Words

geography	change	region
location	culture	contour
migration	scale	topography
distribution	legend	hachure
maps	natural landscape	cultural landscape
direction symbol	title	

Student Activities

1. Where can you find the scale on Figure 1?
2. How many cities are on Figure 1? Which one of the cities is the largest in area? Which city has the most population? How can we find what city has the most people from this map?
3. Which town has the greatest number of roads and railroads running through it (Figure 1)?
4. Find three rivers or streams on Figure 1. Which river is the largest? What town does it flow through?
5. Name the states which border Arkansas. How many states have a common boundary with our state?
   Is Arkansas located in the center of the United States? Why is it important to be centrally located?
7. In which direction are the following states located from Arkansas? California, New York, Louisiana, Colorado.
8. Locate your county and the town where your school is located. What direction is Little Rock from your county and town? (Figure 8)
9. According to the legend on Figure 8, how many people live in your town?
10. Name two of Arkansas' largest towns as given on Figure 8.
11. What is missing on this map which would show how one could travel from one town to another? (Figure 8)

Selected References

De Blij, H. J. *Geography: Regions and Concepts*. 2nd ed. New York: John Wiley & Sons, 1978.

Haggett, Peter. *Geography: A Modern Synthesis*. 3rd ed. New York: Harper & Row, 1972. (see Chapter 1)

Jordan, Terry G., and Rowntree, L. *The Human Mosaic: A Thematic Introduction to Cultural Geography*. New York: Harper & Row, 1979. (see Chapter 1)

Lanegran, David A., and Palm, Risa. *An Invitation to Geography*. New York: McGraw-Hill, Inc., 1973. (see Chapter 1)

McDonald, J. R. *A Geography of Regions*. Dubuque, Iowa: William C. Brown, 1972.

Murphy, Rhoads. *The Scope of Geography*. 2nd ed. Chicago: Rand McNally, 1973. (see Chapter 1)

Taaffe, Edward J. *Geography*. Englewood Cliffs, N. J.: Prentice-Hall, 1969. (see Chapter 1)

Other Sources

County Highway Maps of Arkansas, Arkansas Highway Department, Little Rock, Arkansas.

Topographic Quadrangle Maps, Arkansas Geological Commission, Little Rock, Arkansas.

Chapter 2

THE HYDROLOGIC CYCLE

Arkansas' physical environment includes the features and nature of the earth's surface, atmosphere and climate, land forms and soil, water and mineral resources, and the distribution of plants and animals. As you can see, the **physical environment** is of utmost importance to man since it includes everything surrounding and affecting the development of plants and animals, including man. It also provides a base for the activities of man and provides the air we breathe, the water we drink, and the soil in which most of our food is grown.

Many important activities in the physical environment occur in cycles, just as the seasons repeat themselves each year. One such cycle, the **hydrologic cycle,** or water cycle, is used in this text as a framework to show the connections among the various parts of the physical environment. The hydrologic cycle illustrates the movement of water in the environment. Water and its movement through the environment is very important in determining what grows where. Water is a vital resource that sets a number of important environmental activities in motion. The continuous cycle is sort of like a "merry-go-round" and it keeps the earth supplied with water (Figure 9).

The hydrologic cycle may begin with **evaporation** of moisture into the air from water bodies such as lakes and rivers. Later, this moisture is returned to the earth in various forms such as **rain** and **snow.** When this water falls on the earth it can move in various ways. Some may seep into the soil, some that strikes pavements or rock may **run off** to other areas and some may evaporate back into the air. The water that runs off or seeps into the soil eventually makes its way back to the water bodies in streams above or below the surface of the earth. Thus, the cycle is completed and may begin again.

We will now look at the hydrologic cycle in Arkansas. The hydrologic cycle is largely responsible for the state's climate. The major elements of climate, especially rainfall or precipitation, contribute to the growth of plants and the development of soil. The next few chapters describe and analyze the key parts of this most important water cycle.

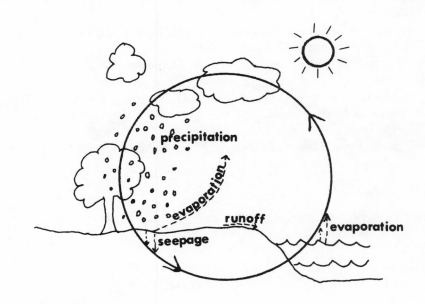

Figure 9. The Hydrologic Cycle.

Key Words and Activities

Key Words

physical environment
hydrologic cycle
evaporation
precipitation
runoff

Study Questions

1. Why is the physical environment vital to man?
2. How is the hydrologic cycle used to study the physical environment?

Selected References

Carter, D. B.; Schmudde, T. H.; and Sharpe, D. M., "The Interface As A Working Environment: A Purpose for Physical Geography," Technical Paper No. 7, Washington, D. C.: Association of American Geographers, 1972.

Hidore, John J. *Physical Geography: Earth Systems.* Glenview, Illinois: Scott, Foresman and Company, 1974.

Leopold, Luna B. *Water: A Primer.* San Francisco: W. H. Freeman and Company, 1974.

Muller, Robert A., and Oberlander, T. M. *Physical Geography Today: A Portrait Of A Planet.* 2nd ed. New York: Random House Publishers, 1978.

Ward, R. C. *Principles of Hydrology.* London: McGraw-Hill, Inc., 1967.

Chapter 3

CLIMATE

Introduction

Climate may be defined simply as long-term **weather** conditions. It is important in understanding an area's physical environment. Arkansas' climate is controlled by two kinds of air: warm, moist air from the Gulf of Mexico and cool, dry air from Canada. In summer, warm, moist air is dominant and rainfall occurs largely from local afternoon and evening thunderstorms produced by the intense heat from the summer sun (Figure 10). During the winter, cold, dry air from Canada invades Arkansas and may collide with warmer, more humid air. These strikingly different kinds of air meet and produce precipitation as they cross the state from west to east (Figure 10).

Temperature

Temperatures during the short winter season are mild and seldom fall below zero (0°F). Summers are long and hot with daily highs sometimes exceeding 100°F in July and August.

Temperatures vary from north to south across Arkansas with average January temperatures ranging from a low of 34°F in the northwest to a high of 42 °F for counties in southern Arkansas (Figure 11). These **average monthly temperatures** are based on average daily temperatures for each day of the month for the last ten years. Average July temperatures vary from 76°F in northwestern Arkansas to 82°F in southern and eastern Arkansas (Figure 12).

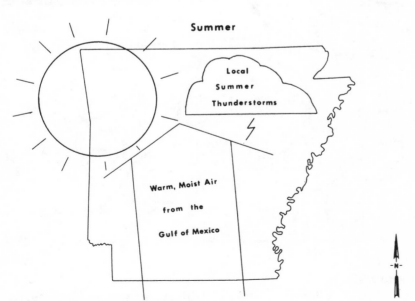

Figure 10. Precipitation in Arkansas.

Source: H. B. Stroud

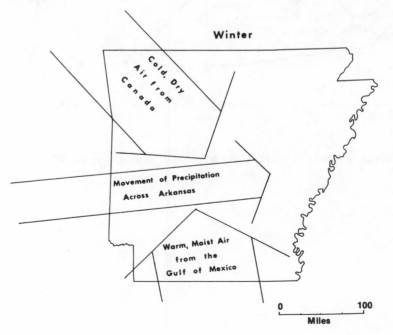

0   100
Miles

13

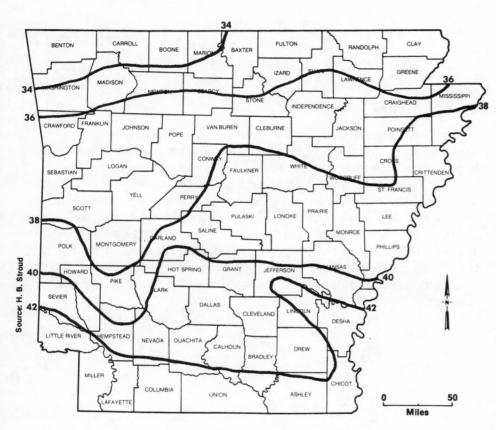

Figure 11.
Average January temperature (°F) in Arkansas — 1969-1978.

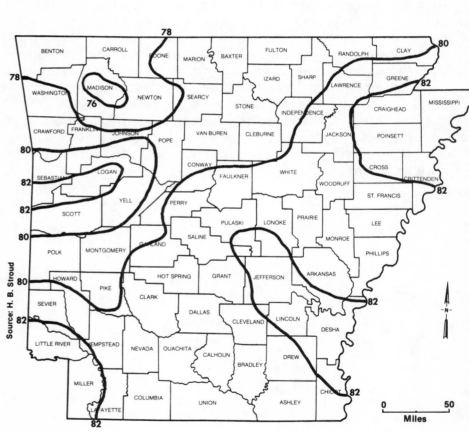

Figure 12.
Average July temperatures (°F) in Arkansas — 1969-1978.

Precipitation

Rainfall occurs as warm moist air from the Gulf rises above colder, drier air to produce much of Arkansas' precipitation. Additional precipitation comes from local thunderstorms in the summer.

Precipitation totals range from a low of 40 inches per year near Fort Smith to a high of 58 inches in small areas in the Ouachita Mountains of western Arkansas. The Ouachitas are more humid than surrounding areas because air is forced to rise over the mountainous terrain. As warm moist air rises, it cools and precipitation is often released because the waterholding capacity of cooler air is less than for air with higher temperatures. Air with a high moisture content may yield precipitation with only slight amounts of cooling.

In general, rainfall amounts increase from the northwest to the southeast across Arkansas. Northern counties receive 44 to 52 inches of precipitation while counties in southern and eastern segments receive from 48 to 56 inches of rainfall per year (Figure 13). The greatest amount of rainfall usually occurs during the months of March, April, and May, with the driest periods coinciding with the warm temperatures of July, August, September, and October.

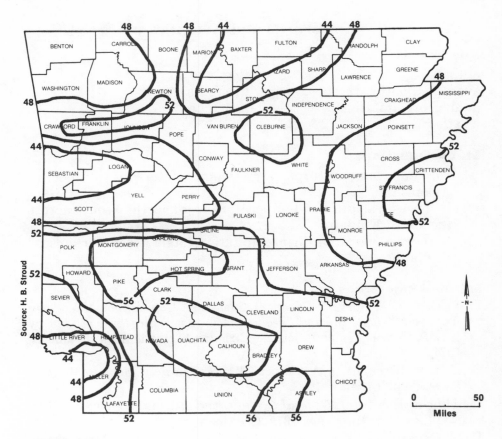

Source: H. B. Stroud

Figure 13.
Average annual precipitation (inches) in Arkansas — 1969-1978.

Climatic Hazards and Uncertainties

Climatic patterns and weather conditions are much less predictable and much more uncertain when viewed on a short-term basis. An examination of daily or seasonal weather conditions will reveal occasional periods of **flooding, droughts,** and **tornadoes.** These hazards are a particular problem for Arkansas during certain periods of the year. Tornadoes and floods may occur during any month but are most likely during the spring. Droughts are most likely during late summer and fall. These periods of water shortage have been few and brief.

While floods have caused much damage, the destruction from tornadoes has been much more severe. Arkansas is one of 15 states in an area that is the most likely to experience tornadoes and ranks fifth in the total number of tornado occurrences. Unfortunately, the state also ranks high in the number of killer tornadoes. While no months are completely tornado free, peak months of tornado occurrence are March, April, and May.

Key Words and Activities

Key Words

climate   flooding
average monthly temperature   droughts
annual precipitation   tornadoes
weather

Study Questions

1. How do temperatures vary from winter to summer in Arkansas?
2. Is there a variation in temperature from north to south across the state? Explain.
3. Is there a variation in precipitation totals across Arkansas? Explain.

Selected References

U. S. Geological Survey, Arkansas Geological Commission. *Floods in Arkansas, Magnitude and Frequency Characteristics through 1968*, by J. L. Patterson. Water Resources Circular 11, Little Rock, Arkansas, 1971.

Cole, H. S. "Drought In Arkansas," *Weather Bureau Monthly Weather Review*, Vol. 61, May, 1933.

Critchfield, Howard J. *General Climatology*. 3rd ed. Englewood Cliffs, N. J.: Prentice-Hall, Inc., 1974. (see Chapter 1)

U. S. Department of Commerce, National Oceanic and Atmospheric Administration. *Climate of Arkansas*. National Climatic Center, Asheville, N. C., October, 1976.

U. S. Department of Commerce, National Oceanic and Atmospheric Administration. *Climatological Data: Annual Summary, Arkansas*. Washington, D. C.: Government Printing Office, 1969-1978.

U. S. Department of Commerce, National Oceanic and Atmospheric Administration. *Outstanding Tornadoes in Arkansas*. National Weather Service Forecast Office, North Little Rock, Arkansas, January, 1979.

Chapter 4

TOPOGRAPHY

Arkansas' topographic surfaces range from mountains in the north and west to the flat lands of eastern Arkansas. **Topography,** the shape and form of the earth's surface, is important in determining whether the precipitation falling on Arkansas runs off at the surface in streams or seeps into the soil.

Topography is also one of the most distinctive features that gives character to places. It is important in the formation of soil and influences such activities of man as settlement, agriculture, transportation and recreation. Certain types of terrain are suitable for agriculture (those areas where slopes are gentle) while other types of topography are more desirable for settlement or for recreation. Mountainous terrain, for instance, is most desired by many for numerous recreational activities, including snow skiing, hiking, and mountain climbing.

The topography of Arkansas may be divided into upland and lowland areas. The uplands generally are found in the western and northern segments of the state and the lowlands occupy much of southern and eastern Arkansas. Arkansas' upland area is generally referred to as the **Interior Highlands** and the lowlands as the **Gulf Coastal Plain.**

The Interior Highlands has two major divisions: the **Ozark Mountains** (Plateaus) and the **Ouachita Mountains** sections. The **Arkansas Valley** is also within the Interior Highlands grouping and is located along the Arkansas River between the Ouachita Mountains and the Ozarks. **Crowley's Ridge** is also included as highland even though commonly considered as part of the **Mississippi Alluvial Plain.**

The lowlands of Arkansas are occupied by the **West Gulf Coastal Plain** of southwestern Arkansas and the **Mississippi Alluvial Plain** (commonly referred to as the Delta) of eastern Arkansas.

The exact location of these topographic surfaces and the surface irregularities associated with each are presented on a relief map of Arkansas (Figure 14). This map gives a visual impression of the irregular nature of the Ozark Mountains and the Ouachita Mountains, the gently rolling hills of southern Arkansas and the flat surface within the Mississippi Alluvial Plain. Crowley's Ridge is also visible as an area of irregular hills within the otherwise flat Alluvial Plain. The six major topographic divisions presented here provide the basis for the establishment of the six natural regions in Arkansas that are presented in Chapter 8.

Key Words and Activities

Key Words

topography

Study Questions

1. Why is topography an important part of the hydrologic cycle?
2. What are the major topographic divisions in Arkansas?
3. Can you describe the topography of the region where you live?

Selected References

Arkansas Department of Planning. *Arkansas Natural Area Plan.* Little Rock, Arkansas, 1974.

Fenneman, N. M. *Physiography of the Eastern United States.* New York: McGraw-Hill, Inc., 1938.

Fisk, H. M. *Geological Investigation of the Alluvial Valley of the Lower Mississippi River.* U. S. Army Corps of Engineers, 1944.

Foti, Tom. *Arkansas: Its Land and People.* Arkansas Department of Education, Environmental and Conservation Office, Little Rock, Arkansas, 1976.

Saucier, R. T. "Quaternary Geology of the Lower Mississippi Valley," *Arkansas Archeological Survey,* Research Series No. 6, 1974.

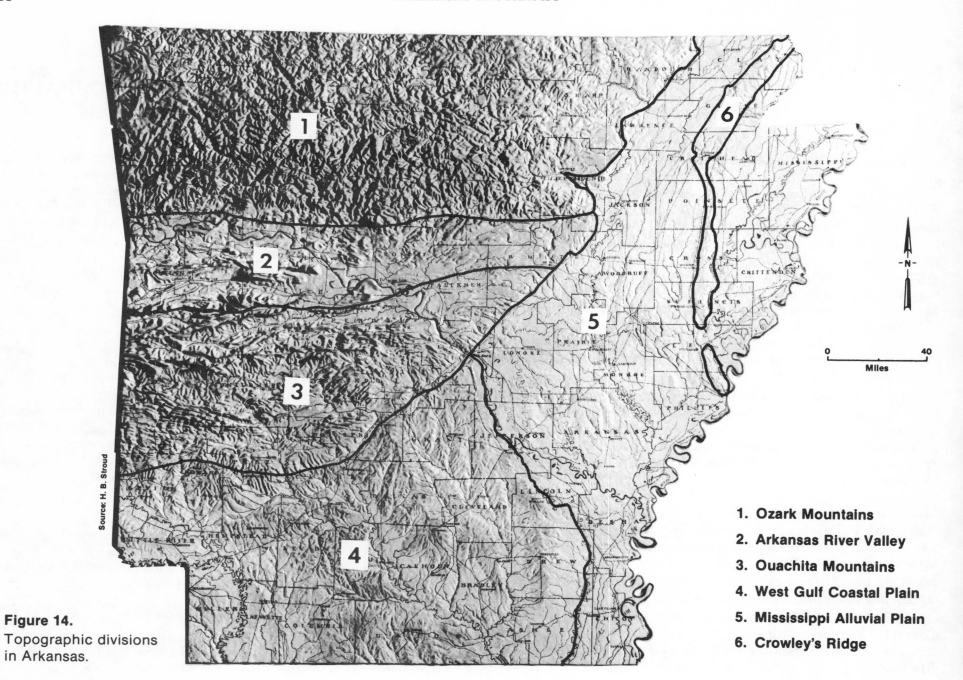

Figure 14.
Topographic divisions
in Arkansas.

1. **Ozark Mountains**

2. **Arkansas River Valley**

3. **Ouachita Mountains**

4. **West Gulf Coastal Plain**

5. **Mississippi Alluvial Plain**

6. **Crowley's Ridge**

Source: H. B. Stroud

Chapter 5

VEGETATION

The **natural vegetation** for Arkansas is trees. Trees and forests are found in all but a few areas where prairie grasses dominate. Forests cover more than half the land in the state and over 17 million acres can be used for growing industrial timber. How large is an acre?

It is important to remember that the original vegetation of many portions of the state has long been removed. The areas where forests predominate are found west of the Mississippi Alluvial Plain and include a southern section where pine predominates and a northern section where oak-hickory is the dominant type.

Much of eastern Arkansas has been cleared for agricultural purposes, with most forests being limited to wetland (poorly drained) areas. The oak-gum-cypress is the most important type. Crowley's Ridge provides an important exception because of its higher elevation, greater slope, and poorer soil. Here the **Upland Hardwood Forest** types are found. **Prairie** as the natural vegetation type is now limited to the Grand Prairie of Arkansas in Prairie and Lonoke counties and other scattered areas in Franklin, Logan, Sebastian and Benton Counties and small plots in Ashley, Bradley, Drew, and Hempstead Counties.

Vegetation in Arkansas can be categorized into four major types that are found in distinctive patterns largely coinciding with natural or physiographic boundaries. Major types include **Loblolly-Shortleaf Pine, Upland Hardwood** (oak-hickory), **Bottomland Hardwood** (oak-gum-cypress) and **Prairie** or **Nontyped** (less than 10 percent forest) (Figure 15). Each of these major vegetation types has many different kinds of trees and grasses. These types will be examined more closely in Chapter 8. Which forest-type do you have in your region?

As is obvious from Figure 15, the Loblolly-Shortleaf Pine type is largely concentrated in Southwestern Arkansas and represents

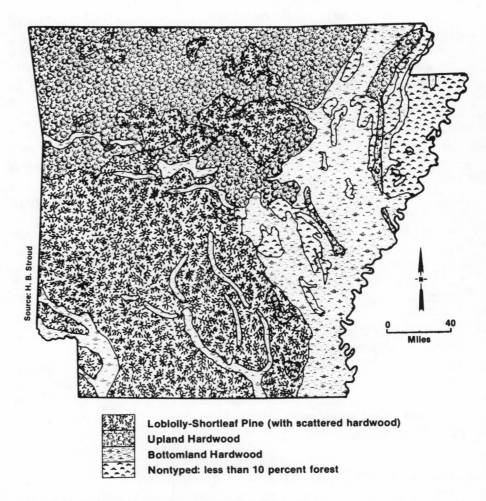

Source: H. B. Stroud

▨	Loblolly-Shortleaf Pine (with scattered hardwood)
	Upland Hardwood
	Bottomland Hardwood
	Nontyped: less than 10 percent forest

Figure 15. Major forest types in Arkansas.

the dominant land use within the West Gulf Coastal Plain and the Ouachita Mountains natural regions. Sizable acreages of this forest type are also found in the Arkansas Valley in Johnson and Pope Counties and in the Ozark Mountains in Van Buren and Cleburne Counties and in several smaller stands scattered across northern Arkansas within the Ozarks.

Upland Hardwoods (oak-hickory) are extensive throughout the Ozarks and in parts of the Arkansas Valley. Crowley's Ridge is also covered by Upland Hardwoods with only extremely limited areas of Upland Hardwoods on the Alluvial Plain or in the Southwest.

Bottomland Hardwoods are limited to eastern Arkansas and along streams in the Arkansas Valley and in the Gulf Coastal Plain. Eastern Arkansas also has extensive areas that are classified as Prairie or Nontyped where trees occupy 10 percent or less of the total land area.

Forests, like those described above, are an important part of the hydrologic cycle and help determine rates of infiltration and runoff. A well-vegetated surface, such as a forest, slows the rate at which precipitation strikes the surface. Rain droplets hit the leaves and limbs of trees and then drip to the surface much more slowly than for non-vegetated areas. The forests also provide a litter of leaves, twigs, and nuts that covers the forest floor. This litter absorbs a great deal of precipitation. The tree roots also provide openings for the infiltration of water. These three factors provide conditions that almost never produce direct surface runoff in a forest.

Because of the large forest regions, Arkansas has vast areas where infiltration is good and soil erosion is not a particular problem. The areas that are unprotected or under cultivation are much more likely to yield surface runoff and erosion. Soil loss is very small in an oak forest but increases substantially for row crops cultivated downslope. This tremendous increase in soil loss shows how important vegetation cover is in preventing direct surface runoff and soil erosion.

Key Words and Activities

Key Words
natural vegetation

Study Questions
1. What role does vegetation play in the hydrologic cycle?
2. What are the major vegetation types in Arkansas?
3. What happens to rain which falls in the forest? What happens to rain which falls on pavement or concrete?

Selected References

Arkansas Forestry Commission. *Forestry: Its Economic and Environmental Importance to Arkansas*. Little Rock, Arkansas, 1972.

Trewartha, Glenn T.; Robinson, Arthur H.; and Hammond, Edwin H. *Physical Elements of Geography*. New York: McGraw-Hill, Inc., 1967.

U. S. Department of Agriculture, Forest Service. *Arkansas Forest Resource Patterns*. Southern Forest Experiment Station, Resource Bulletin SO-24, New Orleans, Louisiana, 1970.

Chapter 6

SOILS

Arkansas **soils** range from those that are thin, rocky and not very productive to deep and highly productive stream-deposited soils. What kind of soil do you have in your region? The varying soil types have strikingly different rates of soaking up water and are important in the hydrologic cycle.

The size of the soil particles and how closely they fit together are two of the most basic physical properties of the soil and are important in determining the amount of open space in the soil and the rate at which water moves through the soil. For example, **sand** has relatively large particles that produce a soil with relatively large openings or void spaces. These large openings allow for the rapid movement of water.

Clay, on the other hand, has small particles and small openings between soil particles. These small openings retard the movement of water and, as a result, water moves through these clayey soils very slowly. Many areas of clay soil have poor drainage and where slopes are gentle are likely to contribute to the formation of **wetland areas,** as in eastern Arkansas, for example.

The formation of soil goes on all the time but so slowly that it is not noticeable. Soils cover much of the earth's surface and are continuously being modified by developing into thicker more mature soil or by being eroded away. The soil mantle, while appearing to be static and unchanging, is dynamic and full of life.

The Soil Conservation Service has divided the soils of Arkansas into 12 different soil groups. The complex variety of soils in Arkansas coincide largely with major topographic divisions of the state or are found in patterns that roughly parallel major streams. These soils vary from those that have formed over mountainous terrain to those bottomland and terrace types.

For the purpose of this text, the 12 soils are simplified and reduced to 6 major categories by grouping the Ozark Highland soils, by combining the Boston Mountains and Arkansas Valley soils and by eliminating those soils that are limited in areal extent, such as the Cherokee Prairies and the Blackland Prairie soils (Figure 16). The six major groups are: **1. Ozark Highlands, 2. Boston Mountains/Arkansas Valley, 3. Ouachita Mountains, 4. Forested Coastal Plain, 5. Bottomland and Terrace,** and **6. Loessial.**

Ozark Highland Soils occupy large areas of northern Arkansas with the Boston Mountains/Arkansas Valley grouping extending across a large segment of western Arkansas north and south of the Arkansas River. Ouachita Mountain Soils coincide with mountainous terrain of the Ouachitas and are predominant in several counties south of the Arkansas Valley and north of the West Gulf Coastal Plain.

The Forested Coastal Plain Soils occupy much of southern Arkansas while the Bottomland and Terrace Soil type occurs along major streams and most particularly along the Red, Ouachita, Saline, Arkansas, Black, Lower White, and Mississippi river valleys. Loessial Soils are wind deposited soils and are found in several areas of eastern Arkansas particularly along and on either side of Crowley's Ridge. Finally, the Eastern Prairie Soils (mapped as loessial soils) occur within the Grand Prairie of eastern Arkansas on nearly level terrain in Arkansas and Prairie Counties.

Erosion, sediment yields, and soil loss are important considerations for the various soil types. Sediment is a major pollutant of lakes and streams. It reduces esthetic values, destroys recreational potential, interferes with navigation, destroys fish and wildlife habitat, and reduces the life of water supply and flood control reservoirs.

Sediment yields and severe erosion occur at varying rates across the state. Erosion is more of a problem near construction sites and is a particular problem along new road construction and within major land development projects. There are several ways of reducing erosion and sedimentation and these methods should be required by those who may disrupt the soil.

Key Words and Activities

Key Words

soil	erosion
sand	Loessial Soils
clay	sediment yields
wetlands	soil loss

Study Questions

1. What are the major soil types in Arkansas?
2. How do soils affect the movement of water in the environment?

Selected References

Portland Cement Association, *PCA Primer*. Skokie, Illinois: Engineering Bulletin, 1973.

Soil Association Map of Arkansas. U.S. Department of Agriculture, Soil Conservation Service, Little Rock, Arkansas, 1967.

Steila, Donald. *The Geography of Soils*. Englewood Cliffs, N.J.: Prentice-Hall, Inc., 1976.

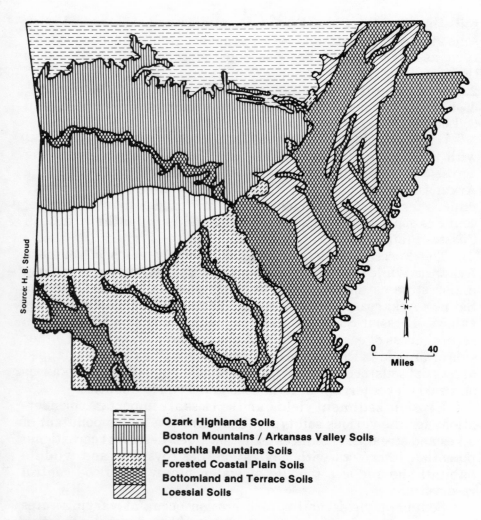

Source: H. B. Stroud

Ozark Highlands Soils
Boston Mountains / Arkansas Valley Soils
Ouachita Mountains Soils
Forested Coastal Plain Soils
Bottomland and Terrace Soils
Loessial Soils

Figure 16. Major soil types in Arkansas.

Chapter 7

WATER RESOURCES

Arkansas has a vast water resource base. It has a dense **drainage network** and an enormous ground water supply in some areas. These water resources are supplied largely by precipitation from the hydrologic cycle. Unfortunately, much of this water is not available for use by man. Some of the water is too deep below the surface, large amounts are polluted, and some is tied up in the atmosphere in vapor form.

Stream Flow

Arkansas' dense drainage network can be divided into five major **drainage basins** or **watersheds** (Figure 17). A watershed is the area drained by a major stream and its **tributaries,** which are smaller streams or rivers that flow into the large one. The Arkansas River is a tributary of the Mississippi, for example.

The greatest volume of water in Arkansas moves through the Arkansas and White Rivers, respectively. The other major rivers are the St. Francis, the Ouachita and the Red. These five rivers empty into the Mississippi River. The Mississippi flows along Arkansas' eastern border and is the largest river in the United States.

Streams flow from higher to lower elevations following the path of least resistance. This water moves toward the stream's mouth where it may empty into a larger stream or into a lake or ocean. Streams in Arkansas flow southeastward across the state from the highlands of northwestern Arkansas to the lowlands of the eastern and southern segments of the state.

The five major river basins within the boundaries of Arkansas may be ranked according to size. The ranking is based on the amount of water moving through each basin. The **Arkansas River Basin** has the greatest volume of flow with 38 percent of the total for

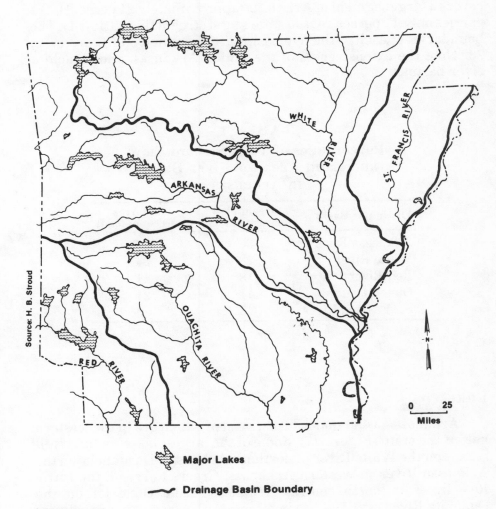

Figure 17.
Major streams, drainage basins, and lakes in Arkansas.

23

the state (Table 1). The **White River Basin** is second with 29 percent while the **Red, Ouachita,** and **St. Francis** basins have 18, 11, and 5 percent of the total stream flow, respectively.

Even though the Arkansas River Basin has the greatest volume of stream flow, it occupies only 25 percent of the state's total land area. The White River Basin covers the largest area, occupying 34 percent of the state's land area. The Ouachita River Basin also covers a large segment of Arkansas (approximately 21 percent), but carries only 11 percent of the state's total stream flow (Table 1). The boundaries of each of the five basins are presented on Figure 17, p. 23. Note the extensiveness of the White, Arkansas, and Ouachita river basins.

TABLE 1
Percentages of Total Stream Flow and Land Area for River Basins in Arkansas

Drainage Basin	Stream Flow (percent of total)	Land Area (percent of total)
Arkansas River	38	25
White River	28	34
Red River	18	11
Ouachita River	11	21
St. Francis River	5	9

Lakes

Arkansas has 30 major lakes, most of which are in the western half of the state (Figure 17). Some of the largest lakes include Bull Shoals on the White River in northern Arkansas, Dardanelle on the Arkansas River in western Arkansas, Greers Ferry on the Little Red River in north central Arkansas, Lake Ouachita on the Ouachita River near Hot Springs, and Millwood on the Little River north of Texarkana.

Ground Water

There is a highly variable amount of water below the land surface of Arkansas. This water is commonly referred to as **ground water** and is found at varying depths below the surface depending on the nature of the underlying rock structure. Underlying rock types are also important in determining the amount of ground water available for a particular region. Eastern Arkansas is fortunate to have an underlying geologic structure suitable for vast amounts of water storage. Other parts of Arkansas have smaller amounts of water below the surface. Rocks below the surface of much of western and northern Arkansas have limited open space for water storage and as a result wells produce relatively small amounts of water. The variation in well production is presented in Figure 18. Much of eastern and southern Arkansas has wells that produce more than 500 gallons of water per minute. Wells on Crowley's Ridge, in southwestern, and in northern Arkansas produce moderate amounts of water (50-500 gallons per minute). Lowest amounts occur throughout central and western Arkansas.

Summary

The preceding chapters, having considered the major components of the physical environment, have illustrated the complexity of Arkansas' terrain, soils, vegetation, and water resources, and has shown what an important role each plays in the hydrologic cycle. Variations in terrain, such as differences in topography, can tell us a great deal about the usefulness of the land. Soils have different characteristics and allow the seepage of water at different rates. Vegetation serves as a protective cover for the surface of the earth and is important in preventing direct surface runoff and erosion. The movements of water through the environment and the major factors controlling its movement have been emphasized. You must understand these movements of water and the changes they cause in order to fully understand how the environment functions.

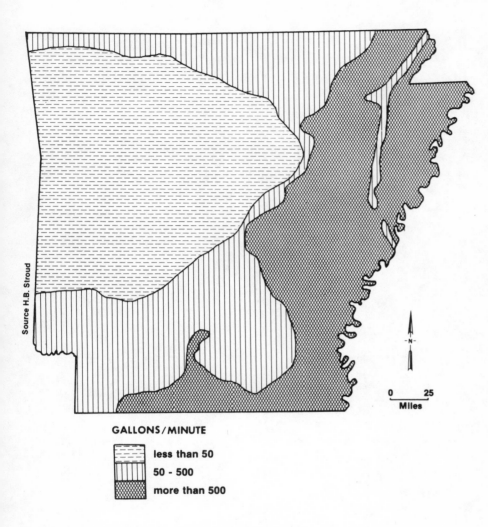

Figure 18. Groundwater well yields in Arkansas.

Key Words and Activities

Key Words

drainage network
drainage basin
ground water
tributary

Study Questions

1. Would you assess Arkansas' water resources as vast or limited? Explain.
2. Is there a surface lake (dam) in your home county? How is it used?
3. What are some positive and negative factors associated with damming streams?

Selected References

U. S. Geological Survey, Arkansas Geological Commission. *Bibliography and Selected Abstracts of Reports on Water Resources and Related Subjects for Arkansas Through 1976.* Water Resources Summary Number 10, Little Rock, Arkansas, 1976.

U. S. Geological Survey. *Ground-Water Levels in Observation Wells in Arkansas.* Water Resources Division, Little Rock, Arkansas, Spring, 1979.

U. S. Geological Survey, Arkansas Geological Commission. *Use of Water in Arkansas, 1975.* Water Resources Summary Number 9, Little Rock, Arkansas, 1977.

U. S. Geological Survey, Arkansas Geological Commission. *Water For Arkansas* by R. T. Sniegocki and M. S. Bedinger. Little Rock, Arkansas, 1969.

U. S. Geological Survey, Arkansas Geological Commission. *Water-Supply Characteristics of Selected Arkansas Streams.* Water Resources Circular Number 9, Little Rock, Arkansas, 1965.

Water Facts of Arkansas. Arkansas Industrial Development Commission, Little Rock, Arkansas, June, 1968.

Chapter 8

NATURAL REGIONS OF ARKANSAS

The regional concept is important in geography and has many useful applications. **Regions** are used to describe some part of the earth's surface and an endless number can be established. When we discuss the conflict in the Middle East, farm problems in the Corn Belt, or rainfall in the Amazon Basin, we are using the regional concept as a general frame of reference. Regions based on the activities of man are referred to as cultural regions and may be defined as portions of the earth's surface where certain cultural traits prevail.

Regions may also be established based on the location of physical elements or environmental features. These so called **natural regions** coincide with a particular kind of topography (mountains for example) and have a distinctive rock type, soil, vegetation, and climate. Arkansas actually may be divided into six natural regions including the **Mississippi Alluvial Plain, Crowley's Ridge, West Gulf Coastal Plain, Ouachita Mountains, Arkansas River Valley,** and the **Ozark Mountains.** Reading about each of these natural regions will enable you to better understand how the various parts of the state differ (Figure 19).

Mississippi Alluvial Plain

The eastern portion of Arkansas has a unique physiography. Here the Mississippi Alluvial Plain, often referred to as the "Delta," is bounded on the east by the Mississippi River, on the southwest by Gulf Coastal Plain and on the northwest by the Ouachita Mountains and the Ozark Mountains (Figure 19).

This region stands alone because of its flat surface and because of the dominance of surface features created by the work of large streams. The Alluvial Plain is flatter than any other region in the

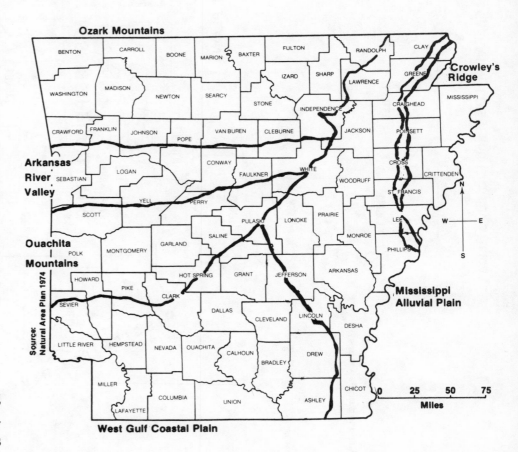

Figure 19. Natural regions of Arkansas.

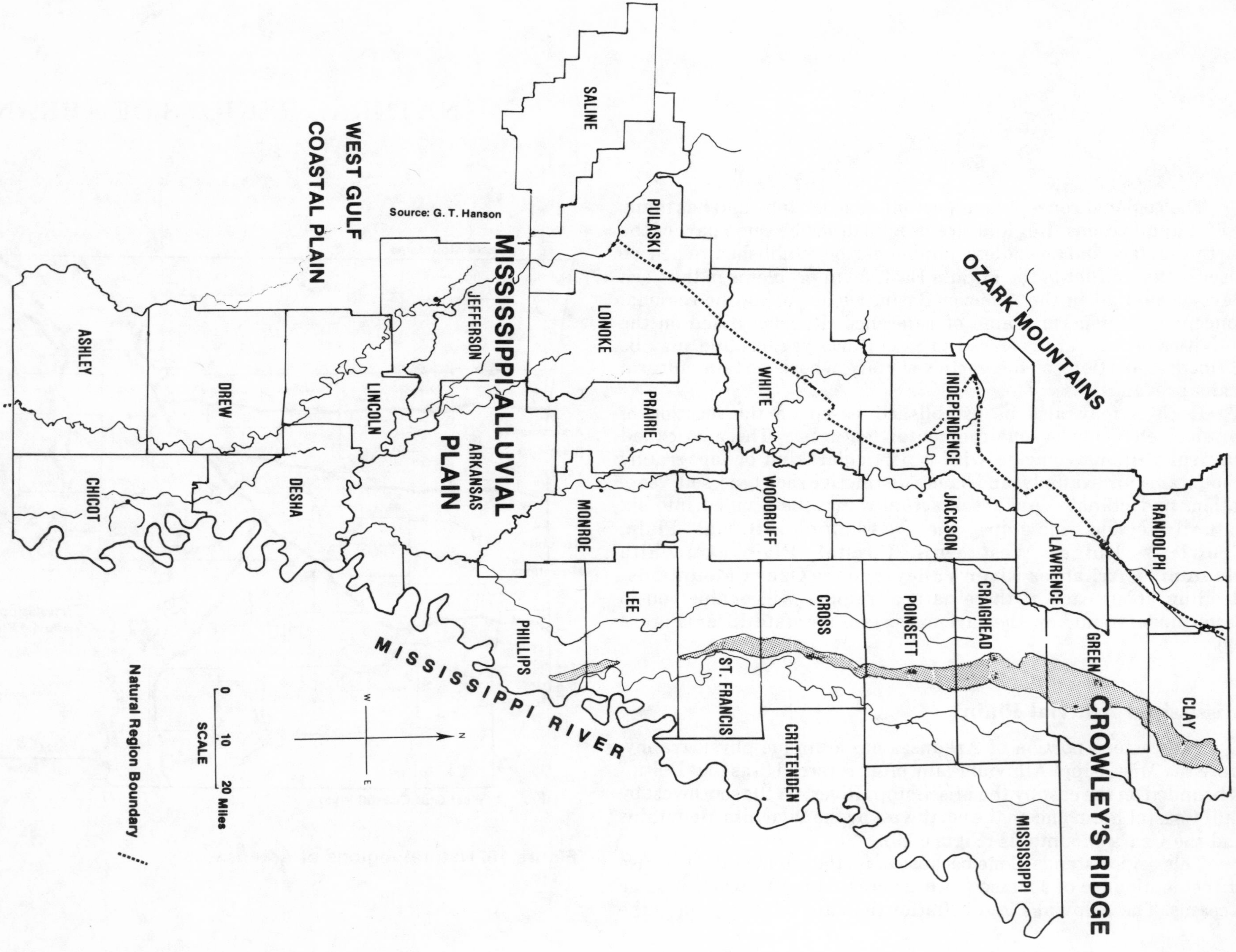

Figure 20. Mississippi Alluvial Plain and Crowley's Ridge.

state with elevations varying only about 150 feet in the entire 250-mile length of the division (from Missouri on the north to Louisiana on the south).

The work of large rivers has been dominant in forming the character of the land. The Arkansas, White, St. Francis, Mississippi, and even the Ohio at one time have flowed through this region. They cut away older deposits and built up deposits of sand, gravel, and clay transported from slopes as far away as the Rocky Mountains in the west and the Appalachians in the east. These streams have produced, in poorly drained areas, a terrain and soil most suitable for large farms. In fact, this region is noted as one of the most agriculturally productive regions in the world.

Alluvium (stream deposited material) and **terrace deposits** cover almost all of the region. Terraces are flat areas frequently found paralleling streams but are slightly elevated above the surrounding stream banks. Terrace deposits are frequently older than present bottomlands and represent former levels of bottomland below which streams have now cut. The recent alluvium has been deposited over the last two million years and contains waterwashed materials, especially silt.

The soils in this region are deep but often so dense that water does not seep through easily, causing poor drainage in many areas. The flat land and poor drainage produces many wetland areas. The broad alluvial plains of certain segments of eastern Arkansas are capped with wind-deposited silt. These wind deposits are particularly large on the west side of Crowley's Ridge. Most of these deposits are deep and have clay subsoils.

Eastern Arkansas also has areas of **Prairie Soils** primarily found in Arkansas and Prairie Counties. This area is the Grand Prairie, where the terrain is nearly level and the clay subsoils are generally compact.

The region has a distinctly different vegetation cover than that of the other lowland division, the Gulf Coastal Plain. The Alluvial Plain has various bottomland hardwoods that are adapted to the wet, poorly drained soils. The **loblolly pine** is absent in this region with the **cypress-tupelo-gum types** occupying the wettest sites. These sites have not been extensively cut over because they are hard to reach. The willow oak and the overcup oak-water hickory occupy flat and poorly drained sites. Much of this type is poor timber.

Higher bottomland and terraces have willow oak and sweet gum types on poorly drained sites. Oak-hickory occupies higher, better drained sites of the **flood plain**. The flood plain is the area which floods when the stream overflows its banks at various times of the year.

In summary, this natural region has several distinguishing characteristics, including its level terrain, wetland areas, large farms and agricultural significance, deep alluvial soils, and widely-scattered **Bottomland Hardwood** forests.

Crowley's Ridge

Crowley's Ridge, while sometimes considered part of the Mississippi Alluvial Plain, has many distinctive features. The Ridge is an area of hills ranging in width from 1 to 12 miles and extending for about 200 miles from southern Missouri through eastern Arkansas to Helena (Figure 20). There is a slight break in the Ridge at Marianna.

Crowley's Ridge is completely surrounded by the Mississippi Alluvial Plain and can be easily seen because it rises some 250 feet above the flat flood plain. This rolling to hilly region is covered with wind-deposited material **(loess)**)that is similar to the bluffs along the Mississippi River in western Tennessee. It is also distinctly different in that its forests are more closely related to the tulip tree-oak forest of the Tennessee hills and other areas to the east than to the oak-hickory forest of the Ozarks to the west.

The vegetation of Crowley's Ridge is actually very rich in the number of species. Trees vary from the lowland forest type found along streams to upland forest consisting of post oak-black jack oak and black oak-hickory on exposed, poorer sites of the Ridge proper. North slopes and deep gullies contain a forest type more closely related to that of the western Appalachian Mountains than to any type found elsewhere in Arkansas.

Crowley's Ridge is also distinctive in terms of its land use. Much of the region is in woodland with extensive areas of pasture. Row crops such as soybeans and wheat are limited almost entirely to small flood plains along streams that flow out of the region onto the Alluvial Plain. One reason for limited agricultural activity is the erosive nature of Crowley's Ridge soils. Crowley's Ridge soils must, in many instances, have a protective vegetation cover of some type if severe soil erosion is to be prevented.

West Gulf Coastal Plain

The Gulf Coastal Plain is an area of relatively gently sloping terrain extending across the southern segment of the United States from Texas to Georgia. This is an area that was covered by the waters of the Gulf of Mexico until about fifty million years ago. The region was covered by a vast sea when the land area was lower than it is today. As the land rose, water in the Gulf of Mexico retreated to near its present position. During the last million years, the level of the coastline has fluctuated at various times. During glacial advances much water was locked up in glacial ice and the coastline shifted farther south. Much of what is now the **continental shelf** was exposed as dry land. However, when the glaciers melted, much more water flowed into the oceans and the coastline advanced northward toward Arkansas. Because it was covered by the ocean for much of its history, the Coastal Plain is flat to rolling, its bedrock is deeply covered with sediments, and the surface is often gravel.

The western portion of the Gulf Coastal Plain extends across southern Arkansas and has been named the West Gulf Coastal Plain. This plain is found south of the Ouachita Mountains and extends southward to the \Gulf and eastward to the Mississippi Alluvial Plain. The boundary between the West Gulf Coastal Plain (usually referred to simply as the "Coastal Plain") and the Ouachita Mountains is the boundary between the more recent deposits of the Plain and the older rocks of the mountains.

The two areas have strikingly different topographic surfaces. The slopes separating the mountains from the Coastal Plain are often so steep that there are rapids or waterfalls at points where streams leave the mountains. The term **"fall line"** has been used to describe the boundary.

The eastern boundary of the West Gulf Coastal Plain is the Arkansas River from Little Rock to Pine Bluff and the Bayou Bartholomew from Pine Bluff to the Louisiana border. These two rivers separate the West Gulf Coastal Plain from the recent alluvial deposits of the Mississippi Alluvial Plain (Figure 21).

The most distinctive features of the region are its extensive **loblolly pine forest**, level to rolling terrain, deposits of sand and

gravel, industrially significant deposits of clay, bauxite, and petroleum, and deposits of wind-blown soil (loess). Despite its level to rolling terrain and areas of rich soil, it is a region dominated by forests and forestry activities. Both pine and hardwood products are harvested in this region where the forest industry is particularly significant. Agricultural activities are limited to pasture land, truck farming, and limited field crop production along more fertile valleys adjacent to the major streams that flow through the region.

The Coastal Plain, with its surface deposits that are of ocean-bed origin, dates back some 135 million years. Generally, the surface materials are poorly consolidated sand and clay with scattered deposits of lignite and small amounts of quartzite and limestone. Bauxite deposits are found in Pulaski and Saline Counties in the surface material, with oil and natural gas deposits located in older and deeper formations below the Coastal Plain. There are also industrially significant deposits of clay near the surface.

The region contains predominantly **Forested Coastal Plain Soils** except along streams where **Bottomland and Terrace Soils** are found. The Gulf Coastal Plain is a region of relatively deep soils which are made up of a mixture of sand and silty clay. Soils are reddish, yellowish, or brownish in color. The Coastal Plain of southwest Arkansas has scattered prairies where prairie soils are found.

A mixed forest covers much of the Gulf Coastal Plain. **Loblolly** and **shortleaf pine** species are the most abundant but oak trees are found scattered throughout the pine forest. Bottomland Hardwood forests interrupt this mixed vegetation along the major streams flowing through this region. The major difference between this region and the Ouachita Mountain region is the much greater concentration of shortleaf pine in the Ouachitas.

The loblolly pine occupies a wide range of sites and occurs pure, or in a mixture with, numerous hardwood types. Various mixtures are present throughout the southern part of the state. The oak-hickory-gum type occurs on the best sites of southern Arkansas with the willow-oak type occupying flat, poorly drained soils.

This region, with its rolling topography and extensive areas of forest, is distinctive because its forest industry provides more than 50 percent of the state's total wood production. Land use is

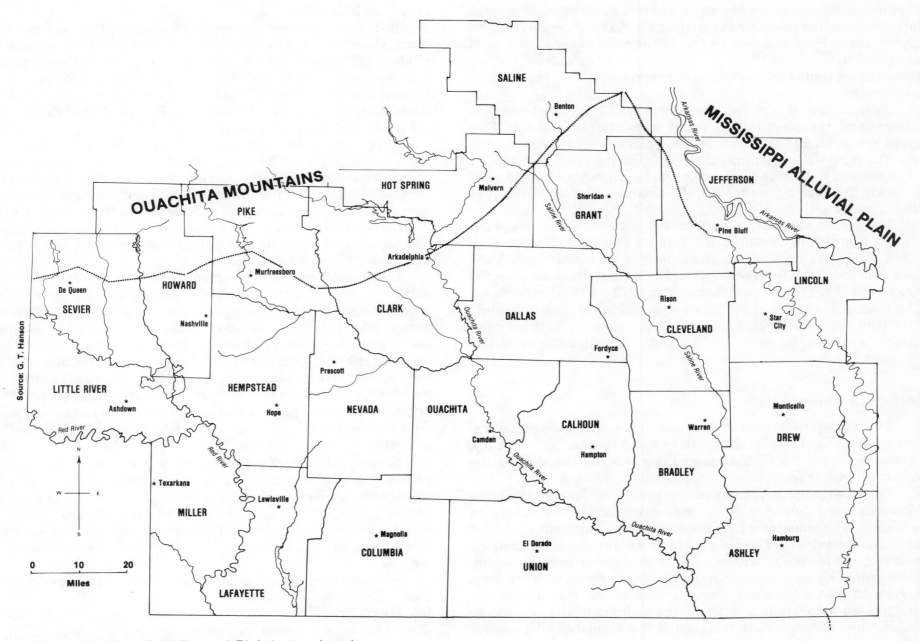

Figure 21. West Gulf Coastal Plain natural region.

dominated by the forest industry where timber companies own large tracts of land totaling approximately 2.58 million acres in this region alone. Forest occupy 70 percent or more of the land area of most counties. More than 120 wood-related industries employ thousands of people and provide a tremendous boost to this region's economy.

Agriculture is limited mainly to cattle production with pastureland representing the major agricultural land use. Row crops are limited to the more fertile valleys along streams.

The region also has important oil-producing land, particularly in Union and Columbia Counties on the Louisiana border. Oil companies in this region produce 20 million barrels of crude oil per year that is worth billions of dollars.

The region also has the only known crater of diamonds in the United States. The prospect of finding a diamond attracts thousands of visitors each year to the Crater of Diamonds State Park near Murfreesboro in Pike County. The largest diamond found at this site since the park was established in 1972 is a 16.37 carat stone. The diamond was found in 1975 and is valued at approximately $100,000. Clay deposits are also of value, especially to brick companies, and are found in Hot Spring, Hempstead, and Miller Counties.

Ouachita Mountains

The Ouachita region, which stretches across west-central Arkansas, is bordered on the north by the Arkansas River Valley, on the south by the Gulf Coastal Plain, and on the east by the Alluvial Plain (Figure 22).

The most notable feature of the region is that the Ouachita Mountains are folded and consequently unlike any others in Arkansas. The mountains here are long ridges which run east-west through the region. The long narrow ridges are separated by relatively wide valleys which may be 20 miles or more in width. Each valley has a stream or river flowing through it. Note from Figure 22 just how many streams flow to the east and south. Imagine an automobile trip from Arkadelphia to Hot Springs to Russellville. This ride up the ridges and down into the valleys would tell you that you are crossing the ridge and valley landforms of the Ouachita Mountains.

Rocks in the Ouachita region are also different from those found elsewhere in Arkansas. Most rocks there are **sandstone** and **shale** which were formed many millions of years ago from sand and mud particles. These particles were cemented together on the bottom of a sea. Eventually the compressed sand and mud layers were squeezed into folded mountains. It is the folded ridges of the Ouachitas which remain today.

There are several differences between sandstone and shale rock. Sandstone is light brown or tan in color and is found in thick layers. Shale rock is usually dark brown or gray in color and is in thin layers and often breaks into fine pieces. Another type of rock found in the Ouachitas region is **novaculite**. Novaculite is a hard rock found around Hot Springs that was once mined by the Indians. The hardness of novaculite made it an excellent material for arrowheads, stone axes, and blades.

Little difference occurs among the Ouachita Mountain soils across the region. Sandstone and shale are the major rocks from which the soils form. These rocks give a light brown or reddish brown color to the soil. Mountain soils are very thin on ridgetops and along steep slopes. Because rains and gravity have been washing the soil particles downhill for many thousands of years, soils in the narrow valleys are much thicker. The soils are not very rich because there are few decayed plants available in the soil. The greatest amount of plant material comes from pine needles, which do not make for a fertile soil. For this reason, Ouachita Mountain soils are poor farming soils.

Several different types of vegetation are found in the Ouachita region. The most common type is the **shortleaf pine forest**. These trees cover much of the region and are especially dense on the slopes and ridgetops. Pine trees grow best where there are thin, sandy soils which are well drained. The pine needles which drop off the trees also make the soils very acid, and other plants do not grow well.

A second type of vegetation found in the Ouachita region is the **Bottomland Hardwood forest**. These trees grow in the valleys on flat, poorly drained land. Willow oak, sweet gum, and water oak are among the most common hardwoods and are often found along the Ouachita, Saline, and Red River valleys.

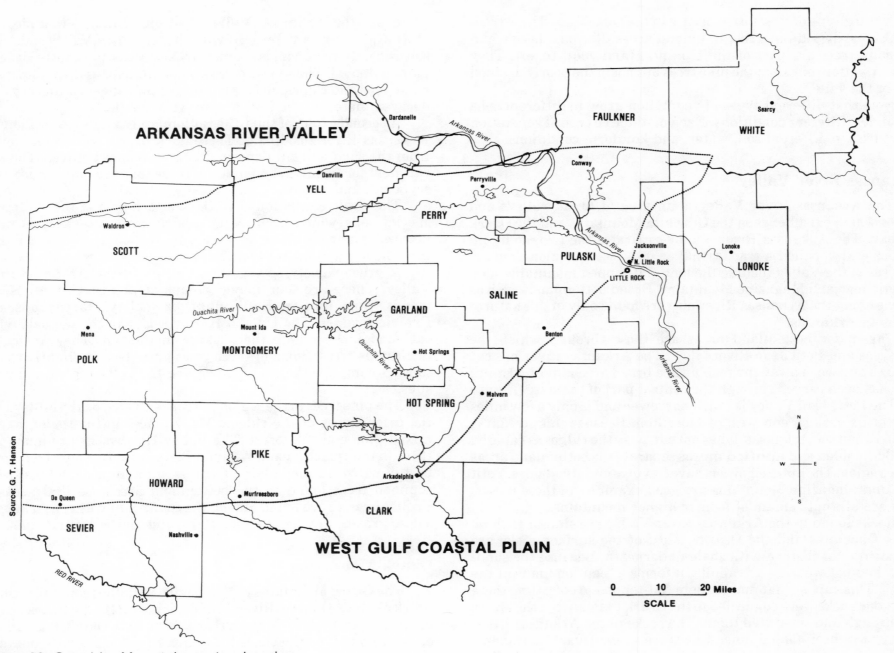

Figure 22. Ouachita Mountains natural region.

A third type of vegetation occurs in the Ouachitas. These trees are also hardwood but grow in upland areas. Red oak, beech, and magnolia trees are part of the **Upland Hardwood forest.** They grow in wetter soils than the pine trees but not in the poorly drained soils of the valleys.

Note that different types of vegetation grow in different soils and under different conditions. Each distinctive type of vegetation grows best in different soil, water, and landform conditions.

Arkansas River Valley

The Arkansas River Valley is an area of broad valleys and ridges which exist between the Ouachita Mountains and the Ozark Plateau. The Arkansas River Valley separates the two mountain regions and is called a transitional or in-between region. Unique features of the Valley include the long flat-topped mountains such as Petit Jean and Magazine Mountains. Broad bottomlands such as the one along the Arkansas River also are found only in this natural region in Arkansas.

The major bottomland areas are those through which the Arkansas and Petit Jean Rivers flow. The Arkansas River has cut through and worn away the rock until a broad area almost 40 miles wide has been carved through the central part of the state (Figure 23). The Petit Jean Valley is much narrower and is only a few miles wide at its eastern end west of Morrilton. Because this stream is smaller than the Arkansas, it has not cut away the ridges as rapidly.

Both folded and **uplifted mesas** separate the bottomland areas in the region. The uplifted mesas have flat tops and steep sides. Petit Jean and Magazine Mountains are good examples of these mesas. They are all that remain of former higher mountains.

Rocks found in the Arkansas River Valley are similar to those of the Ouachitas and the Ozarks. Most of the surface rocks are composed of sandstone with shale underneath. Because the sandstone does not wear away rapidly, it forms a "cap" on many of the ridges. This cap is what makes them flat-topped. At one time these sandstone rocks were connected to the Ozark Plateau, but the rivers cut through and separated them. The rocks in the Arkansas River Valley have been folded much like those in the Ouachita region.

There are three types of soil in the Arkansas River Valley.

These are the **Arkansas Valley, Bottomland,** and **Prairie** soils. Most of the region is covered with the Arkansas Valley soils. This soil is made from sandstone and shale rocks plus some decayed plant material. The soils are light brown in color and are thin on the ridge tops and slopes. Because they are thin and contain very little decayed material, the soils are not very fertile.

A second group of soils, the Bottomland soils, is found along the Arkansas River floodplain. These dark brown soils come mainly from the sand and silt deposited by the Arkansas River. They are excellent for farming, and much of these soils are planted in cotton, soybeans, and wheat.

The Prairie soils found in the western part of the Valley are special soils which occur with prairie grasses. There is much decayed plant material in these soils, which gives them a dark brown color and makes them very rich.

A great variety of vegetation exists in the Arkansas River Valley. There are four major groups of plants: **Upland Hardwoods, pine forests, Bottomland or Valley Hardwoods,** and **Prairie grasses.** The Upland Hardwoods, like the red oak, white oak, and hickory, lose their leaves in the fall. They are called **deciduous** trees. Some of these trees grow best in slightly wetter soils. Others, like the oaks, are best suited to the higher and drier sites.

The pine trees in the region are concentrated on the hilltops and the drier slopes of the ridges. Many places in the region have a mixed pine and oak forest. The Valley Hardwoods are much like those in the Ouachita and Alluvial Plain regions. These trees grow best in wet or flooded plains. Cypress, gum, tupelo, and pecan are common trees found in the bottomland areas. Several areas of Prairie grasses are found among the counties of western Arkansas. These grasses are usually found growing on the Prairie soils.

Ozark Mountains

The Ozark Mountains region begins with the mountains which overlook the Arkansas River Valley (Figure 24). The Ozark region continues north into Missouri and west into Oklahoma. On the eastern side of the Ozarks is the Ozark Front. Here the mountains and hills end abruptly and the flat land of the Alluvial Plain begins.

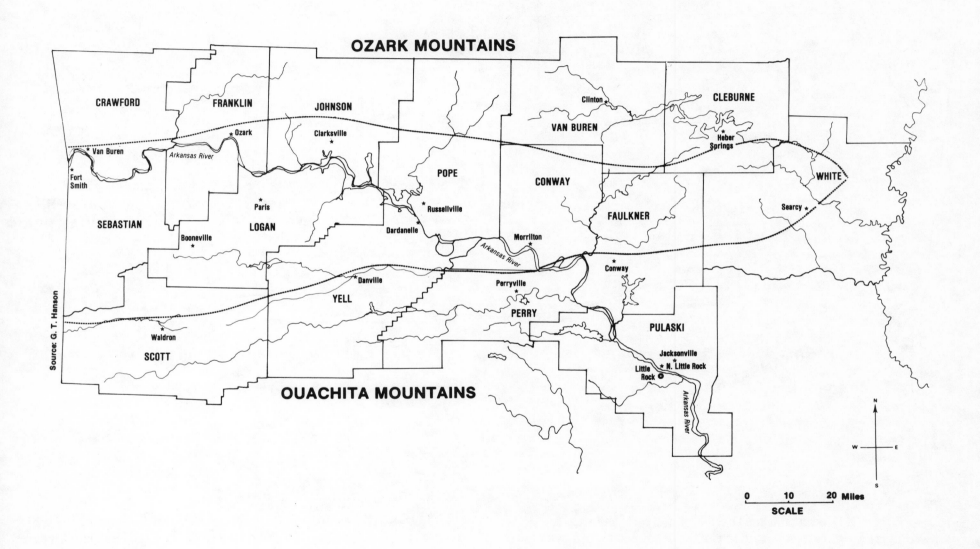

Figure 23. Arkansas River Valley natural region.

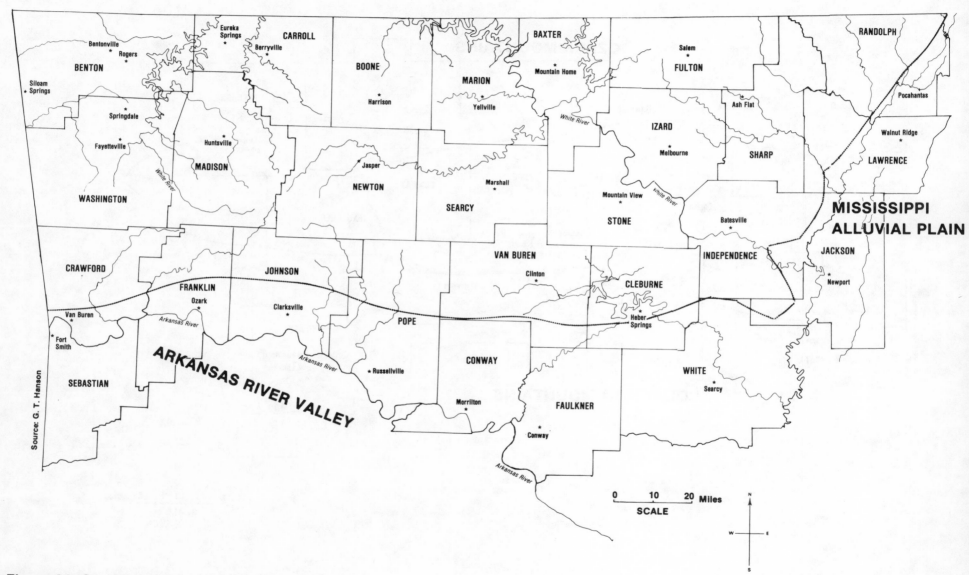

Figure 24. Ozark Mountains natural region.

Landforms within the Ozarks include flat-topped mountains, V-shaped valleys, and many small streams. The Ozark Mountains are really plateaus which have been worn away by water and wind. These plateaus with their flat tops give a special look to the landscape. There usually is a small creek flowing through the valley below. The streams which are still wearing away the valley walls give the valley steep sides and their V shape.

There are three parts to the Ozark Mountains regions: the **Boston Mountains**, the **Springfield Plateau**, and the **Salem Plateau**. The Boston Mountains are highest and have the narrowest valleys and steepest slopes. To the north of these mountains is the Springfield Plateau. Ridgetops on this plateau are at a similar elevation above sea level. The third section is the Salem Plateau. It is not as high as the other two sections. Part of the plateau extends north into Missouri.

Rock types also differ among the three subdivisions. **Limestone** and **chert** rocks are most common in the Springfield Plateau, while **dolomite** and **sandstone** are widely found in the Salem Plateau. Dolomite is a form of limestone with magnesium. The Boston Mountains contain primarily sandstone and shale rocks. All of these rock materials are sedimentary and many are easily worn away by water and wind.

Ozark soils are clearly the product of rock materials and decayed plant materials from the region. Mountain soils are made up from the sandstone and limestone materials found in the mountains. In addition, the fallen leaves and twigs from the oak and hickory trees make up the decayed plant materials in the soil. A large portion of the Salem and Springfield Plateaus is covered by the **Ozark Highland limestone soils**. Their color ranges from gray-brown to yellow-brown. These soils are found under the Upland Hardwood forest and the prairie regions to the northwest. A smaller portion of the Salem Plateau is covered with the **Ozark Highland sandstone-dolomitic-limestone soils**. These are different from the other highland soils as they come from sandstone rock and occur in mixed hardwood and pine forests.

The Ozarks exhibit a wide variety of vegetation. These include many kinds of hardwoods as well as pine forests and prairie grasses. Much of the Ozark Plateau is covered by an **Upland Hardwood forest**. White oak, red oak and hickory trees occupy the wetter and richer soil while the drier and thinner soils contain black hickory and black oak trees. In the cool, moist ravines, beech and sugar maple trees are found. Some areas contain a mixture of hardwood and pine trees. A small but important prairie grassland exists in the western Ozarks in Washington and Benton Counties. Here the tall grass is the most common vegetation found in the natural state. These grasslands have been cleared for farming, an important activity for inhabitants of these counties.

Regional Differences

Arkansas' natural regions are different in many ways. Landforms in the six regions are not the same. For example, it is only in the Alluvial Plain that flat, alluvial land is the dominant landform. The long narrow ridges of the Ouachitas are unique to that region. Even the Ozarks look quite different from the Ouachitas. Differences like these help us to separate the natural regions.

Soil patterns also vary greatly across the six regions. Because soils are formed from rocks and decayed plant matter, they differ from place to place. Compare, for example, the thin, poor soils of the Ouachita Mountains with the thick, rich soils of the Alluvial Plain. Another striking contrast is the Arkansas River Valley soils and the Gulf Coastal Plain soils.

Variety in vegetation also helps us to see differences among the natural regions. There is a great difference in the pine forests of the Gulf Coastal Plain and the oak-hickory forests in the Ozarks. Alluvial Plain vegetation contrasts from the vegetation of the Ouachitas; the cypress trees look far different from the pine trees of the Ouachita ridges. Remember the reasons for the plant differences. Each group of plants grows best under special soil, water, and landform conditions. As we study the landscape of Arkansas, remember the differences among the natural regions.

Key Words and Student Activities

Key Words

Region
Natural region
Alluvium
Flood plain

Study Questions

1. What is the major way to recognize a natural region?
2. List three features which could be used to identify a natural region in Arkansas.
3. Select one of the six natural regions of Arkansas and write out the major features of that region. Locate the region on the map before you start.

Selected References

Allred, B. W. and H. C. Mitchell. "Major Plant Types in Arkansas, Louisiana and Texas and Their Relation to Climate and Soils." *Texas Journal of Science* (VII, July) 1955, pp. 21-35.

Arkansas Department of Planning. *Arkansas Natural Area Plan.* Little Rock, Arkansas, 1974.

Croneis, Cary. *The Physiography of the Paleozoic Area of Arkansas.* Little Rock: Arkansas Geological Survey Bulletin, 1930.

Dale, E. E. "Literature on the Vegetation of Arkansas." *Proceedings Arkansas Academy of Sciences.* Little Rock, Arkansas, 1963.

Foti, Tom. *Arkansas: Its Land and People.* Little Rock: Arkansas Department of Education, 1976.

Foti, Tom. "The Grand Prairie," *Ozark Society Bulletin.*

Foti, Tom. *The Natural Divisions of Arkansas: A Classroom Guide.* Little Rock: Arkansas, 1976.

Moore, D. M. *Trees of Arkansas.* Little Rock: Forestry Commission, 1972.

Shelford, V. E. *The Ecology of North America.* Urbana: University of Illinois Press, 1963.

Other Sources

Physical Maps, *Atlas of Arkansas*, Department of Planning, Little Rock, Arkansas, 1973.

Topographic Quadrangle Maps, (Arkansas), United States Geological Survey, Arkansas Geological Commission, Little Rock, Arkansas.

PART TWO

CULTURAL GEOGRAPHY

The first portion of this book has emphasized the physical environment. We are now ready to examine man and his activities in the physical environment of Arkansas. Man and his interaction with the natural environment may be referred to as the **cultural landscape.** Man-made changes and how these changes have altered the landscape make up an important subfield in geography — **cultural geography.**

Cultural geography analyzes how the activities of man have changed the land and how these changes have taken place. When man first moves into an area, numerous changes in the natural landscape begin to take place. New settlers build houses, roads, farms and villages. Soon political units such as states, counties, and towns develop as more people move into the region. By looking at how settlement occurred in Arkansas, we can better understand our landscape. What effect would a population **decrease** have upon the landscape?

Cultural geography is also concerned with other activities of man. For example, what are the different ways in which man makes his living? What economic activities occur across the state? Where is farming important in Arkansas? These activities are all part of the cultural landscape.

Chapter 9

INDIAN SETTLEMENT IN ARKANSAS

Indian Settlement before 1600

Indians have lived in Arkansas for 8 thousand years or more. During this period, the landforms have changed very little. However, the climate, plants, and animals have changed substantially during this time period.

Climate has become warmer and more moist. The warmer, more moist climate encouraged a spread of pine trees from the south. This in turn led to changes in the types of animals. These changes in plants and animals were important to the Indians. They were **hunters and gatherers** who depended upon animals and plants for their food. The Indians had to seek new plants and animals as the climate changed. Early Indians did not stay in one place very long and moved about almost weekly. In what sorts of places do you think Indians lived?

Certain settlement sites made better settlements than others (Figure 25). **Bluff sites** were best in the Ozarks. Bluffs were easily defended, well drained, and close to water. Another excellent site was the **natural levee** along rivers. These sites in the Alluvial Plain and Gulf Coastal Plain were slightly higher and not subject to flooding. The levees were close to water and contained hardwood trees which had many uses.

Some sites were avoided by early Indians because of flooding or lack of water. Look at Figure 25 and list the things Indians had to consider when selecting a site.

The northern part of the Alluvial Plain has many sites of former Indian settlements (Figure 26). Indians probably migrated into this area from Ohio by traveling down the Ohio and Mississippi Rivers. These Indians were called **Woodland** Indians and practiced hunting and gathering. Later they developed farming and began to live in permanent villages. These villages were often on **natural levees.**

Indians from Louisiana and Mississippi came in by the way of the southern Alluvial Plain before 1000 A.D. Like the Woodland Indians, these tribes were chiefly hunters and gatherers. By 900 A.D., they had begun to grow beans, corn, and squash. Villages sprang up along the natural levees and temple mounds were constructed.

Southwestern Arkansas also received Indians from Louisiana and Texas. By 100 A.D., permanent Indian villages existed along the Red and Ouachita Rivers. Natural levees again were the favorite sites. The Indians also found the alluvial soils excellent for farming. After 900 A.D., these Indians, called the **Caddo,** lived in distinctive houses, built burial mounds and had a strong tribal government. The Caddoan way of life spread slowly into the sparsely inhabited Ouachita Mountains. Perhaps the mountainous environment, with its different plants and animals, was not favored by the Caddo.

The Ozark region did not have many Indians before 1600 A.D. Indians wandered into the area from Kansas and Missouri to hunt and gather. They did not settle here permanently, however, and used the bluff caves along the rivers for only a few months before moving on.

The earliest account of the Indians in Arkansas came from Hernando de Soto's visit in 1541. De Soto entered Arkansas from Mississippi with several hundred men looking for gold. His journey provides us with the earliest account of the Indian culture by a European. He traveled through eastern Arkansas, then westward to near Little Rock. The expedition spent the winter near the present city of Camden before leaving the state in 1542. De Soto reported Indians living in permanent villages in eastern and southwestern Arkansas. He also mentioned the types of crops they grew and their hunting and gathering activities. By this time, many Indians had learned to farm and live in permanent villages.

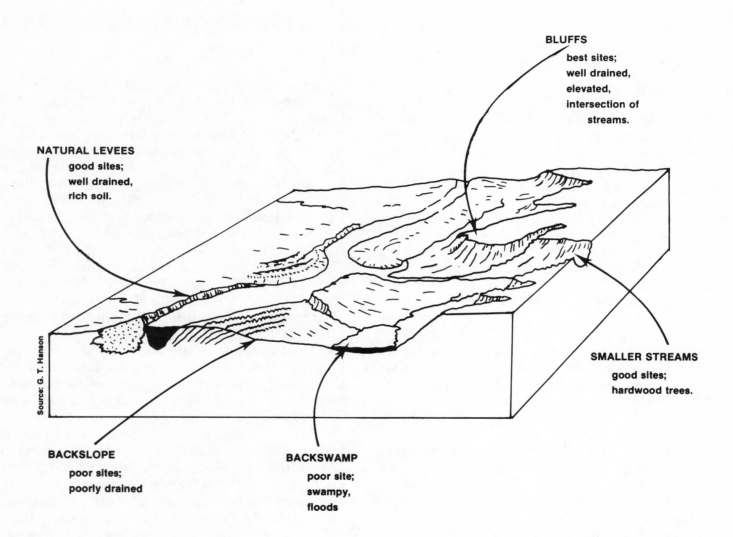

BLUFFS
best sites;
well drained,
elevated,
intersection of
streams.

NATURAL LEVEES
good sites;
well drained,
rich soil.

Source: G. T. Hanson

SMALLER STREAMS
good sites;
hardwood trees.

BACKSLOPE
poor sites;
poorly drained

BACKSWAMP
poor site;
swampy,
floods

Figure 25. Environmental sites for Indian settlement.

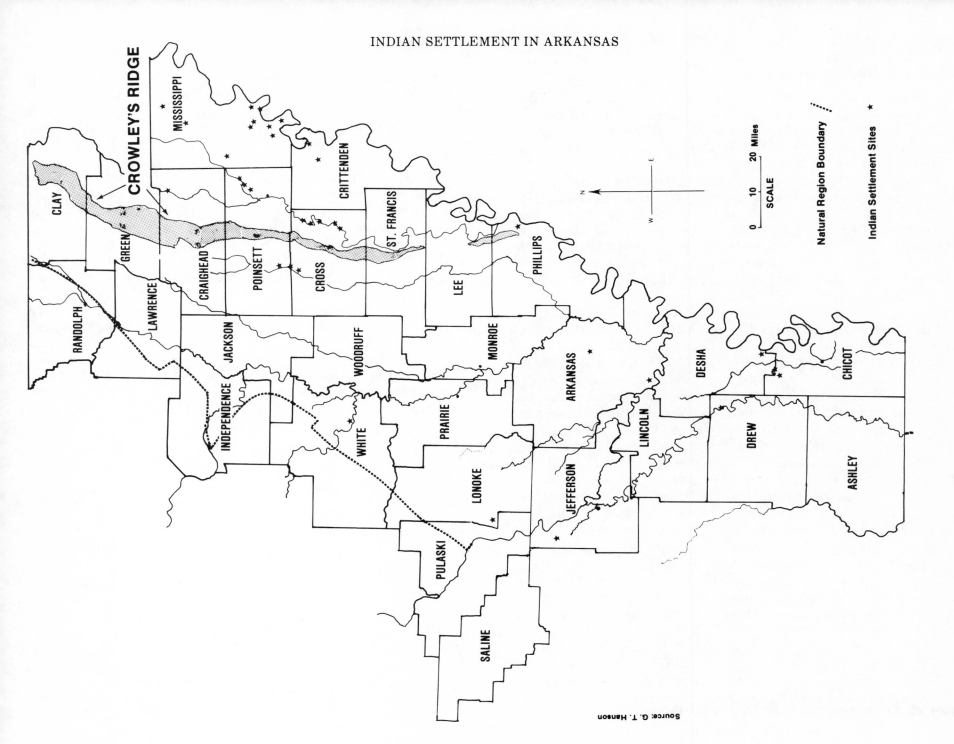

Figure 26. Indian sites in eastern Arkansas.

Indian Settlement after 1600

The coming of the Europeans after 1600 meant a decline in the numbers of Indians. De Soto and later explorers brought in new diseases like whooping cough, measles, and the common cold. Indians, not having an immunity to these diseases, died in large numbers from the illnesses.

There were also other reasons for the collapse of the Indian culture. New tools, different technology, and different ideas came with the Europeans. These new ways did not always fit into the Indian culture. With the coming of the Europeans, land ownership and uses changed. The Indians had never owned land as individuals but used it together with others. Europeans, however, owned land individually and used it without regard to others. The Indians had been self-sufficient, but with the coming of the Europeans, trade became important since the Indians could not make European tools they had come to depend upon. The new settlers arriving from the east feared the Indians and forced the Indians westward.

The settler arriving in 1790 in the area would have found four distinct Indian tribes: the **Osage, Quapaw, Tunica,** and **Caddo** (Figure 27). The Osage lived in northwest Arkansas near the Missouri borderland. They belonged to a larger group of Indians who had come from the Ohio River valley three hundred years before. The Osage were primarily hunters and gatherers who depended upon forest plants and animals for food. They did not raise crops nor did they live in one place for very long.

The Quapaw originally had lived in the eastern United States but moved westward by 1650. When the settlers came in 1790, the Quapaw lived along the lower part of the Arkansas and White Rivers. The Quapaw, or "downstream" people, were farmers and lived in permanent villages along the natural levees of the rivers. These Indians became allies of the French, who reported their life style in great detail. The Quapaw were finally forced out of Arkansas by 1818 and moved westward into Oklahoma.

Only a few score of Tunica Indians lived in Arkansas in 1790. They occupied a small portion of Chicot, Desha, and Ashley Counties in extreme southeastern Arkansas. They also were farming people who occupied permanent villages. Like many of the Indians, they gathered plants and hunted animals to add to their food supply.

The fourth tribe, the Caddo, occupied the southwestern part of the state. The few hundred Caddo who lived in Arkansas in 1790 were part of a larger Indian confederacy in Texas and Oklahoma. They had large villages with huge burial mounds. Farm fields surrounded these sites and were often quite productive. By 1835, all of the Caddo had moved out of Arkansas into Texas.

The Indian culture did not survive in Arkansas because the European way of life forced out Indian ways and people. By 1836 when Arkansas became a state, few Indians remained in the area. They had been forced off their tribal lands and pushed westward into Oklahoma. Despite the peaceful nature of the Indians, new settlers arriving in the area feared the Indians as a threat to the settlers' safety. Through several treaties with the federal government, the Indians lost their land and hunting rights as well.

During the first thirty years of the nineteenth century, Arkansas settlers witnessed many tribes passing through the state on their way to Indian lands west of Arkansas. This is often called the **Trail of Tears.** Many of the Indians belonged to tribes from Florida, Georgia, Alabama, and Mississippi who had lost their land like those Indians in Arkansas. Creek, Choctaw, Cherokee, and Chickasaw were but a few of the Indian tribes.

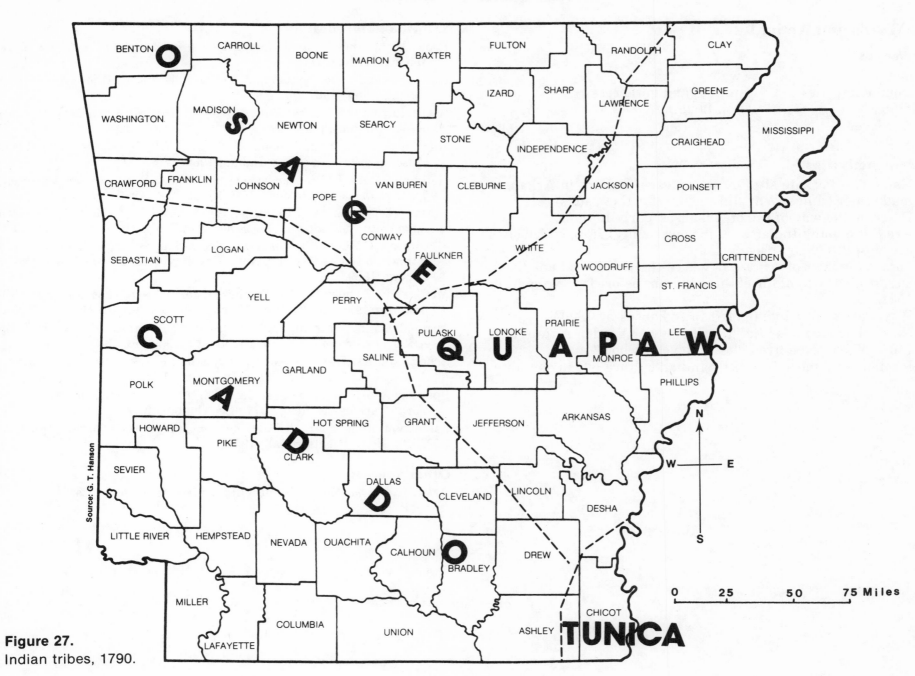

Figure 27.
Indian tribes, 1790.

Source: G. T. Hanson

Key Words and Activities

Key Words

Climate   Swamp
Environmental sites   Hunters and gatherers
Bluff sites   Crop farming
Natural levee

Student Activities

1. Name two favorite sites on which early Indians in Arkansas made their camps. Why did they prefer these sites?
2. Describe the way of life of Arkansas' early Indians.
3. Are there many Indian sites in your county? If so, which sites are closest to your school?
4. Locate the part of Arkansas where the Caddo Indians lived. Describe the way of life of these Indians before De Soto came in 1541.
5. Why were so few Indians left in Arkansas by 1800?
6. Name the four major Indian tribes which lived in Arkansas in 1800. Which tribe lived closest to your school?
7. Explain why there is so little Indian culture left in our state.

Selected References

Broek, J. M. and Webb, John W. *A Geography of Mankind.* New York: McGraw Hill, 1978.

Davis, Hester. "Paleo-Indian in Arkansas," *Arkansas Archeologist.* Vol. 8, no. 1 (Spring) 1967, pp. 1-3.

Gastil, Raymond. *Cultural Regions of the United States.* Seattle: University of Washington Press, 1979.

Harrington, Mark Raymond. *The Ozark Bluff-dwellers.* New York: Museum of the American Indian, 1960.

Hoffman, Michael. "Prehistoric Developments in Southwestern Arkansas," *The Arkansas Archeologist.* Vol. 10, nos. 1-3, 1969, pp. 37-50.

Jordan, Terry G., and Rountree, L. *The Human Mosaic: A Thematic Introduction to Cultural Geography.* New York: Harper and Row, 1979.

McGimsey, C. R. *Indians of Arkansas.* Arkansas Archeological Survey Publication on Archeology. No. 1, Fayetteville: Arkansas Archeological Survey, 1969.

McClurkan, Burney B. "The Culture History of Southeast Arkansas," *The Arkansas Archeologist.* Vol. 10, nos. 1-3 1969, pp. 31-34.

Morse, Dan F. "Introducing Northeastern Arkansas Prehistory," *The Arkansas Archeologist.* Vol 10, nos. 1-3 1969, pp. 13-30.

Scholtz, James. "The Archeology of Northwest Arkansas," *The Arkansas Archeologist.* Vol. 10, nos. 1-3, 1969, pp. 51-60.

Spencer, Robert and Jennings, Jesse D., eds. *The Native Americans.* New York: Harper and Row, 1977. (See Chapter 9).

Zelinsky, Wilbur. *The Cultural Geography of the United States.* Englewood Cliffs, N. J.: Prentice-Hall, 1973.

Other Sources

Arkansas Archeologist. Fayetteville: University of Arkansas.

Chapter 10

MIGRATION AND POPULATION PATTERNS IN ARKANSAS, 1800-1900

Settlement in Arkansas Territory, 1819-1835

Before becoming a state in 1836, Arkansas had been controlled by the Spanish, French, and the United States. In 1819, Arkansas became a territory with the seat of government at **Arkansas Post** located near the Mississippi River in the southeastern corner. The **Territory** consisted of five counties, some of which extended into Oklahoma and Missouri (Figure 28).

Most people lived in isolated cabins far from their neighbors in the Territory. By 1819, there were a few settlements along the **Arkansas, White,** and **Mississippi Rivers.** The population grew slowly from 14,000 people in 1819 to more than 30,000 people in 1836. Thirty-four counties with 40 villages existed at the time of statehood (Figure 29). Compare this map with a modern map of the state and note how many boundary changes have occurred.

The easiest means of travel to Arkansas before 1830 was by river (Figure 30). Many settlers came north on the Mississippi River from Louisiana, then by the Arkansas, White, or Red Rivers into Arkansas. People from the east often traveled south on the Ohio and Mississippi Rivers until they reached the Arkansas or White Rivers. They then traveled upstream into the Territory on these rivers. Although water routes were easiest to travel, some settlers came by land.

The most important land route in the state was the **Old Southwest Trail.** This old Indian trail which had been turned into a military road connected St. Louis with Texas settlements. It passed through Jacksonport, Little Rock, Magnet Cove, and Washington before entering Texas. By 1830, stagecoaches were bringing people into the state. A road also paralleled the Arkansas River from Arkansas Post through Little Rock to Fort Smith. By 1835, two roads had been cut west across the Alluvial Plain from

Memphis and Helena to Little Rock. These routes, however, crossed many bayous and swamps, which made the journey difficult and long. During the spring the roads were often impassable because of floodwaters.

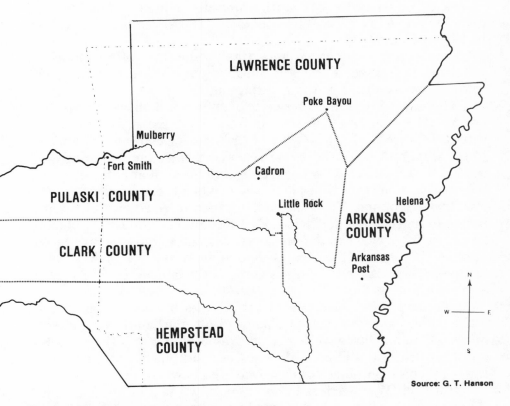

Figure 28. Arkansas territory in 1819.

Antebellum and Post-Civil War Arkansas, 1836-1880

Arkansas began to attract more settlers from the eastern and southern states after 1836. A big attraction was cheap land. In 1836, the Federal government passed the **Homestead Act**. It gave 160 acres of land to each family who would settle on the land. Because Arkansas was a new state, it had many square miles of land to sell. In 1840 Arkansas passed the **Donation Act**, which allowed settlers to obtain forfeited lands. Settlers who failed to pay their taxes forfeited their land back to the state. The Donation Act allowed 160 acres for each member of a family.

Population grew rapidly between 1840 and 1880 (Table 2). Cheap land continued to be the major attraction. Land sold for as little as $1.25 an acre and even at $2.00 an acre it was a bargain. An increase in the number of counties provided evidence of population growth and rising rural settlement. By 1883, seventy-five counties had been formed.

County government expanded as the number of people to be governed increased. Generally larger counties were subdivided into smaller counties as the population grew.

The number of roads increased slowly in Arkansas during this period. This was because road-building was expensive and very difficult. Since the 1820's, steamboats had been coming up both the Mississippi and Arkansas Rivers carrying passengers and freight. Travel by steamboat was hazardous due to sandbars and snags in the rivers. At certain times of the year when the water levels were low, travel stopped. These boats continued to be a very important means of travel until the 1880's. By 1850, almost 3,000 miles of navigable waterways existed in Arkansas, although not all could handle steamboats. Railroad development was slow in Arkansas before 1870. This lack of railroads made the land and water routes even more important.

The Civil War caused a major change in the origins of the settlers who came to Arkansas. Before 1860, most of the people who migrated to our state were from slave-holding states (Figures 31 and 32). Georgia, Alabama, Tennessee, and South Carolina were the most common places of origin for the new settlers.

Pre-Civil War settlers included both white and black people. Many white families coming to Arkansas brough slaves with them.

TABLE 2
Arkansas Population 1810 - 1900

Year	Number of People
1810	1,062
1820	14,273
1830	30,388
1840	95,574
1850	209,897
1860	435,450
1870	484,471
1880	802,525
1890	1,128,211
1900	1,311,564

SOURCE: U. S. Census

Figure 29. Arkansas counties, 1836.

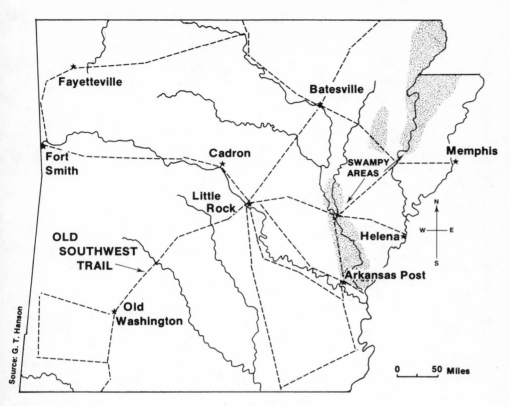

Figure 30. Transportation routes in Arkansas, 1835.

These families generally were cotton farmers seeking land. Many of these settlers sought land in the southern Alluvial Plain region as well as in the Gulf Coastal Plain. Migrants who came to the northern part of the Alluvial Plain and the Ozarks were generally from Tennessee, Kentucky, and Missouri. Most of these settlers did not own slaves.

Between 1860 and 1865, the Civil War made travel difficult and dangerous. In this period migrants came primarily from states east of the Mississippi River. By 1870, however more settlers were arriving from Louisiana, Texas, and even as far away as Illinois and Indiana. Settlers from Louisiana and Texas moved into the Gulf Coastal Plain and the southern Alluvial Plain counties. Those settlers coming from Tennessee, Missouri, and Illinois tended to

settle in the northern Alluvial Plain and Ozark counties. After the Civil War, the number of black people increased rapidly. With the freeing of the blacks in 1863, many former slaves moved westward seeking cheap land on which to farm.

After 1870, new settlers were more likely to come from Missouri, Texas, and Louisiana than from states east of the Mississippi River (Figure 32). States closest to Arkansas were the heaviest contributors of people to the state. As before 1860, most settlers streamed into Arkansas looking for cheap land. The more fertile and level land of the Alluvial Plain and the Arkansas River Valley were eagerly sought.

In 1836, most of Arkansas had a few people. The central Ozarks, northeastern Arkansas, the central Gulf Coastal Plain, and the western Ouachitas were sparsely settled. Gradually more people settled in areas where farming was possible and profitable. By 1880, several areas contained moderate numbers of rural settlers. Northwest Arkansas, the Arkansas River Valley, and the southern half of the Alluvial Plain had farms within sight of one another. Level, fertile land attracted many of these people. Cotton, wheat, and corn were the major crops. With the growth of rural areas, small villages and towns developed in these regions.

The western Ouachitas and Ozarks Plateau regions remained almost uninhabited during the 1836-1880 period. Poor farming conditions were one reason for the sparse settlement and outlaws, another. Gangs of men roamed the area preying upon the settlers. The gangs often fled across the border to the Indian Territory to avoid the law. Judge Isaac Parker, the "hanging" judge of Fort Smith, was often the one who sentenced the captured gang members.

Settlement Patterns 1880-1900

Railroads were not very important in Arkansas until after 1880. Many towns were river towns and those not on the rivers were linked by important roads such as the Old Southwest Trail. Arkansas farmers depended upon steamboats, flatboats, and wagons to ship their crops eastward. As long as farms remained small, the need for railroads to ship produce was not very great.

Railroad development grew rapidly with population increases after 1880. Farmers soon learned that railroads could carry freight

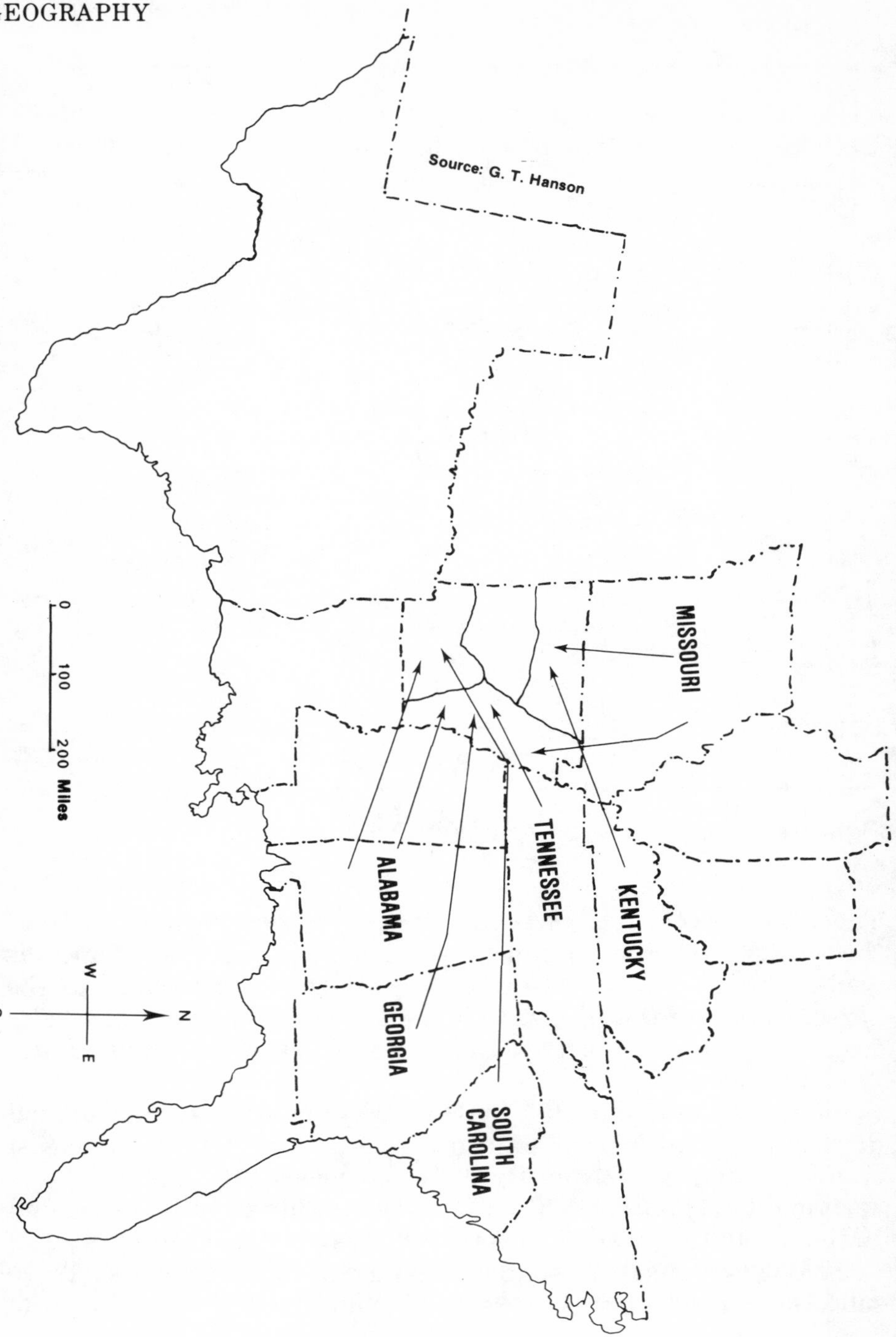

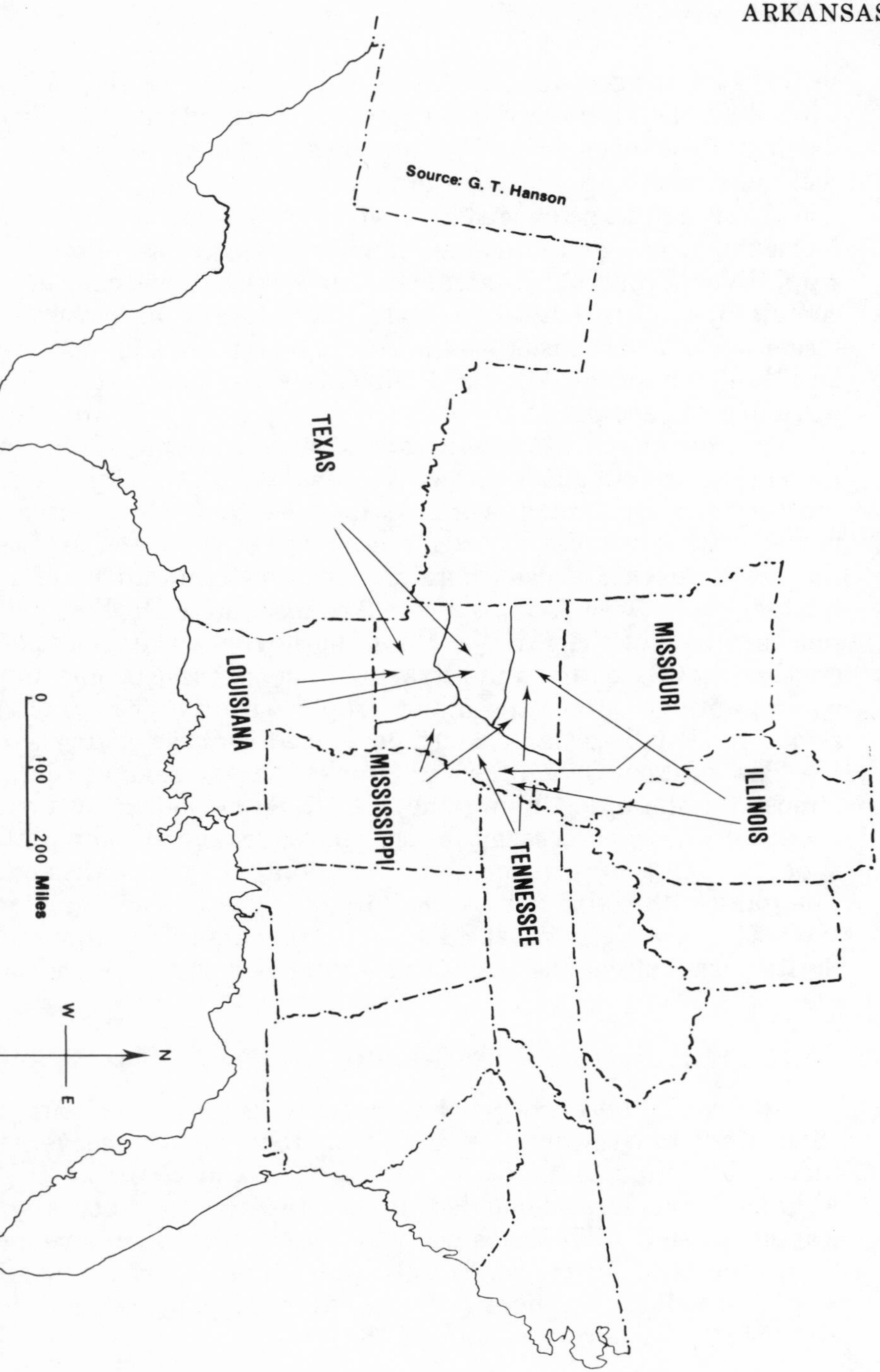

Figure 32. Migration to Arkansas, 1865-1880.

TEXAS

LOUISIANA

MISSISSIPPI

TENNESSEE

MISSOURI

ILLINOIS

Source: G. T. Hanson

0
100
200 Miles

W · S · N · E

Figure 31. Sources of settlers to Arkansas, 1834-1865.

MISSOURI

KENTUCKY

TENNESSEE

ALABAMA

GEORGIA

SOUTH CAROLINA

Source: G. T. Hanson

0
100
200 Miles

W · S · N · E

cheaper and move it faster than river transportation. By 1900, most of Arkansas' farm products were shipped by railroad. Travel also became easier by rail than by stagecoach or steamboat. This made it easier for people to come to Arkansas.

The first Arkansas railroad was begun in 1853 between Madison and Hopefield. The section completed in 1859 was part of a longer Memphis and Little Rock Railroad (Figure 33). The remaining sections between the towns were not completed until 1871. Work was interrupted on the line by the Civil War and frequent floods. Once completed, however, the line provided an important link between Arkansas and Tennessee. With farming in eastern Arkansas becoming more important, the railroad carried much of the corn, wheat, and cotton to Memphis.

The St. Louis, Iron Mountain, and Southern Railroad was completed in 1874. This rail line linked southeastern Missouri with Texas. Note that the railroad runs along the Old Southwest Trail. During the 1880's and 1890's the railroad carried both people and freight to and from Arkansas. The line bordered the Alluvial Plain and Ozark Plateau regions until it reached Little Rock. Towns like Corning, Newport, Beebe, and Cabot grew rapidly with completion of the railroad. Today this railroad is known as the Missouri Pacific.

After 1874, the Fort Smith, Van Buren, and Little Rock Railroad crossed the Arkansas River Valley. The line ran on the north side of the Arkansas River. Note that the railroad paralleled a major land route and a major water route. This railroad with the Little Rock and Memphis line provided transportation across Arkansas. Towns like Conway, Russellville, Clarksville, and Van Buren grew rapidly after completion of the railroad. The rail line also provided sharp competition for the steamboats plying the Arkansas River.

By 1900, eastern Arkansas had several small railroads. The Helena and Iron Mountain Line ran the length of Crowley's Ridge and served Jonesboro, Harrisburg, Wynne, Marianna, and Helena. The line in the heart of the rich farmland gave farmers an opportunity to market their crops to out-of-state areas. Two other railroads, the Little Rock and New Orleans, and the Little Rock, New Orleans, and Pine Bluff also served the Alluvial Plains farmers.

Major railroads which ran east-west across northern Arkansas and the southern part of the state were also finished by 1875. The

North Central Arkansas Railroad was the Ozark's only east-west railroad. It linked Mountain Home with Fayetteville and Van Buren. Southern Arkansas was served by the Mississippi, Ouachita, and Red River line between Eunice and Texarkana.

Arkansas' population increased by 400,000 people between 1880 and 1900. The coming of the railroad was an important reason for continued in-migration of people to the state. Settlements along the railroads grew rapidly after 1880. The railroads meant new trade and more people.

Another change which encouraged population increases was the clearing of land in the Alluvial Plain. Rural population grew along Crowley's Ridge and the northeastern counties during this time. St. Francis, Crittenden, and Craighead Counties all experienced higher rural populations after 1890. Clearing of the hardwood forests encouraged more people to begin farming. Large rural populations were also found in Benton and Washington Counties. Little change occurred in population, however, in the Gulf Coastal Plains and Ouachita Mountain counties by 1900. Farming in these areas was not very successful and settlers avoided moving into the counties.

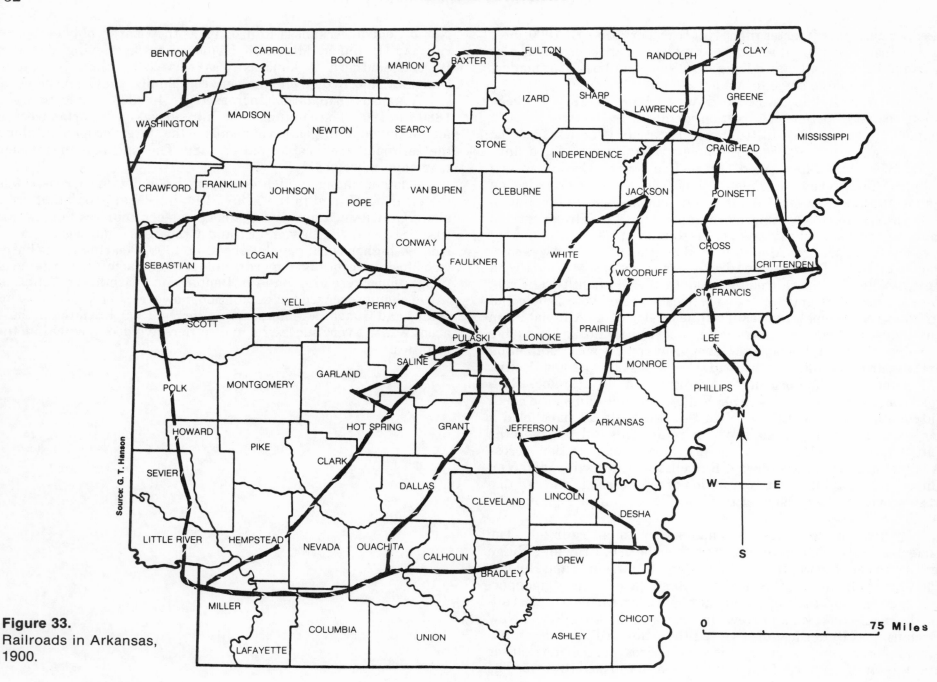

Figure 33.
Railroads in Arkansas, 1900.

Key Words and Student Activities

Key Words

Arkansas Territory	Old Southwest Trail
Statehood	Steamboats
Arkansas Post	Homestead Act. 1836
Mississippi River	Donation Act, 1840
Arkansas River	White River

Student Activities

1. Where did most of the people live in Arkansas by 1836? Why did they live there?
2. Name two important water routes which settlers could take to come into Arkansas. How did many of these settlers arrive in the state?
3. Name some counties and important settlements through which the Southwest Trail crossed Arkansas.
4. Name two other important land routes in Arkansas by 1836. What settlements did these routes connect?
5. What states contributed the majority of the new settlers to Arkansas before 1860? Were these the same states who contributed settlers after 1860?
6. From which states did many of the people who came to your county originate? (Hint: Look at Figures 31 and 32).
7. Locate four major railroads in Arkansas by 1900. What towns did these rail lines connect?

Selected References

Ashmore, Harry S. *Arkansas: A History.* New York: Norton, 1978.

Arkansas Democrat, *Arkansas Centennial, 1836-1936: Commemorating One Hundred Years of Statehood.* Little Rock, 1936.

Dougan, Michael. *Confederate Arkansas.* Tuscaloosa, Ala.: University of Alabama Press, 1973.

DuVall, Leland. *Arkansas: Colony and State.* Little Rock: Rose Publishing, 1974.

Ferguson, John L. ed. *Arkansas and the Civil War.* Little Rock: Pioneer Press, 1965.

Ferguson, John and Atkinson, J. H. *Historic Arkansas.* Little Rock: Arkansas History Commission, 1966.

Herndon, Dallas Tabor. *Centennial History of Arkansas.* Chicago: S. J. Clark, 1922.

Hull, Clifton. *Shortline Railroads of Arkansas.* Norman, Okla.: University of Oklahoma Press, 1969.

Hume, John. "Transportation in Arkansas," *Arkansas Highways.* Vol. X, July, 1978.

Leslie, Jim. *Land of Cypress and Pine: More Southeast Arkansas History.* Little Rock: Rose Publishing Company, 1977.

Leslie, Jim. *Saracen's Country: Some Southeast Arkansas History.* Little Rock: Rose Publishing Company, 1974.

Nuttall, Thomas. *Journal of Travels into the Arkansas Territory during the Year 1819.* Ann Arbor, Mich.: University Microfilms, 1966.

Schoolcraft, H. R. *Journal of a Tour into the Interior of Missouri and Arkansas.* London: 1821. Republished as *Schoolcraft in the Ozarks.* Van Buren: Press-Argus Printers, 1955. edited by Hugh Park.

Thompson, George H. *Arkansas and Reconstruction: The Influence of Geography, Economics, and Personality.* Port Washington, N. Y.: Kennikat Press, 1976.

Walz, Robert. "Migration Into Arkansas 1820-1880: Incentives and Means of Travel," *Arkansas Historical Quarterly* XVII, 1958. pp. 310-324.

Writer's Program, Arkansas. *Arkansas: A Guide to the State.* New York: Hastings House, 1941.

Other Sources

Paullin, Charles O. *Atlas of the Historical Geography of the United States.* edited by John K. Wright. Washington: Carnegie Institution and American Geographical Society, 1932.

Chapter 11

PATTERNS OF POPULATION CHANGE
1900-1980

Pre-World II Changes

The population grew very slowly in Arkansas between 1900 and 1940. There were two million people living in the state by 1940 but only 95,000 people were added to state's population between 1930 and 1940 (Table 3). Population growth was slow for several reasons.

A **rural to urban migration** was occurring during this time. People were moving from farms and country to cities all across the United States and in Arkansas as well. People moved from farms to cities and towns for many reasons. Some sought jobs in the city. Others wanted better houses and schools. In Arkansas, most of the population lived in rural areas. Some people left Arkansas' farms and moved to cities like Little Rock and Fort Smith. Others left Arkansas altogether and moved to St. Louis, Chicago, Los Angeles, Detroit, and other major cities. This resulted in a loss of population for the state.

TABLE 3
Arkansas' Population 1900 - 1980

Year	Number of People
1900	1,312,000
1910	1,547,000
1920	1,752,000
1930	1,854,480
1940	1,949,389
1950	1,909,511
1960	1,786,272
1970	1,923,259
1980	2,279,417

SOURCE: U. S. Census

Another important reason for slow population growth in Arkansas was the Depression. The Depression was a period in the 1930's when many people were without jobs. Without jobs, people could not earn money and many went hungry. The Depression forced many people to give up their houses and land because they could not pay their taxes. With the loss of their houses and land, people often moved away. Arkansas people were especially hard hit by the Depression. Many left the state to seek jobs elsewhere.

A third factor kept Arkansas' population growth low. There were several important changes in farming during this period. These changes included more machines to do the farm work. For example, a single machine such as a grain harvester could do the work of several men. Other machines like tractors, plows, and combines replaced people in the fields. The coming of the machines meant smaller demand for farm laborers, especially in eastern Arkansas where farming was an important economic activity. Machines replaced many thousands of men during this period. The machines were sometimes used to replace men who had moved into the cities. In other instances farmers used the machines because it was cheaper. When this occurred, it forced people to leave the farms and move to cities to seek work.

Finally, the First World War (1914-1918) took men from Arkansas. After the war was over, many of the survivors did not return to the state. Instead they chose to settle elsewhere in the United States. All these factors slowed the population growth in our state between 1900 and 1940.

Not all areas of Arkansas changed population at the same rate during this period. Fourteen counties in the Alluvial Plain region increased in population up to 1930 (Figure 34). One important reason for this growth was the expansion of farming in the Alluvial Plain. Before 1930, much of the land had been covered by swamps and bottomland hardwood trees. Clearing of the land began in the

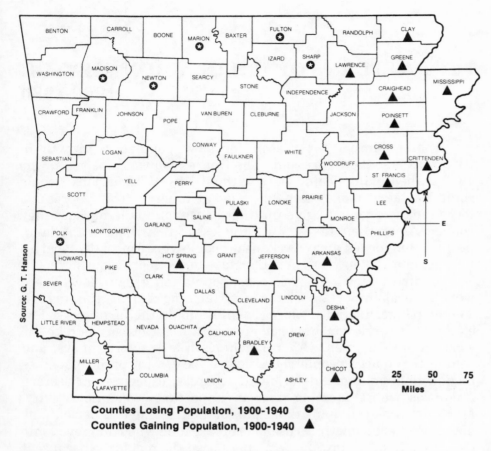

Figure 34. Population changes, 1900-1940.

The Gulf Coastal Plain region slowly gained population every decade from 1900 to 1940. Like the Alluvial Plain however, the Gulf Coastal Plain suffered serious population losses after 1930. The Depression hit the farmers especially hard and many people lost their farms before 1940. Since there were few towns in the region, many people moved to Texarkana or Little Rock.

In the Ouachita region, farming had never been very important and the rural population had always been sparse. When the Depression came after 1930, it did not affect the population of this region as seriously as in the Alluvial Plain. Yet, some counties did lose population between 1900 and 1940. A major reason for the population losses was people moving from the Ouachitas to cities in Arkansas or in other regions or states. The cities of Little Rock, North Little Rock, Fort Smith, and Hot Springs received many of the migrants during hard times.

The greatest losses of population occurred in the Ozark Plateau between 1900 and 1940. During this time, only two of the 19 counties gained population. Only Washington County, where Fayetteville is located, gained people in each decade of the period from 1900 to 1940. Rural population declined in the Ozarks when many people left the county and region entirely. While a few people moved to Fayetteville and Harrison, others went to Little Rock or moved out of Arkansas. Good farming land was found only in Benton and Washington Counties; elsewhere the soils were thin and not very rich. The Depression forced many people to be without jobs in the Ozarks. They were unable to pay their taxes and many were forced to leave their land and houses. Because the Ozarks Plateau area had few large towns, rural people sought jobs in larger cities.

Post-World War II Patterns

Arkansas' population declined very sharply after 1940. From the end of the Second World War until the 1960's, more people died or moved from Arkansas than were born here or migrated to the state. A look at Table 3 (p. 55), shows how serious this loss of population really was. The loss was one of two major population changes to occur in our state during this period. The second change was a sharp increase in population after 1960. What were the reasons for these changes and why did they occur in some areas of the state and not others?

1880's and continued in the early 1900's. This created more farmland, especially east of Crowley's Ridge. The region began to lose its rural population after 1930, however. When the Depression came to the area, farming declined and laborers were unemployed. Losses of population during the 1930's were greatest in the rural areas. All counties in the Alluvial Plain had fewer people in 1940 than in 1930. Most counties had small increases in their city population. This probably means that the people from the rural area were moving to nearby cities.

Let us look at some of the reasons for the losses between 1940 and 1960. The Second World War called away more than 72,000 Arkansans. Some of these men and women died in the war. Others did not come back to the state after the war ended; instead they chose to live in other states. Another factor in the losses was the widespread migration of both white and black people from eastern Arkansas. Many of these people moved to northern industrial cities like Chicago and Detroit where jobs were more plentiful. These employment opportunities attracted many people who had been farm laborers in eastern Arkansas. By 1960 many farms in the Alluvial Plain region had machines to do much of the work. Farm laborers found fewer demands for their services and these people moved to towns and cities. The automobile also contributed to **out-migration**. After 1945, it was easier to travel than ever before. Because of this, people moved more often and farther away than before.

After 1960, new attractions in Arkansas began to reverse the out-migration of people. Fewer Arkansans left the state between 1960 and 1970. More importantly, new arrivals of people started to come from many other states.

What attracted these people? Industries which had formerly been located in northern states moved some of their plants to the South. Arkansas was just one of those states to receive new industries. New industries meant new jobs. Many of these industries chose to move to small towns as well as to the larger cities. A second attraction was Arkansas' climate and physical landscape. Many people wanted to live in a climate which was mild in the winter. They also were looking for a state with hills and lakes for recreation. Finally, the most important source for the population gains was the **in-migration** of retired people. Retired people also sought the mild climate and recreational area opportunities which the state had to offer.

Some parts of the state experienced more losses of population than others (Figure 35). The Gulf Coastal Plain region continued its out-migration pattern begun in the 1930's. Most of the counties lost people between 1940 and 1960. Rural population losses continued in the remaining counties and all experienced rural population decreases up to 1960. With the region's limited farming activity there was little to keep people on the rural land.

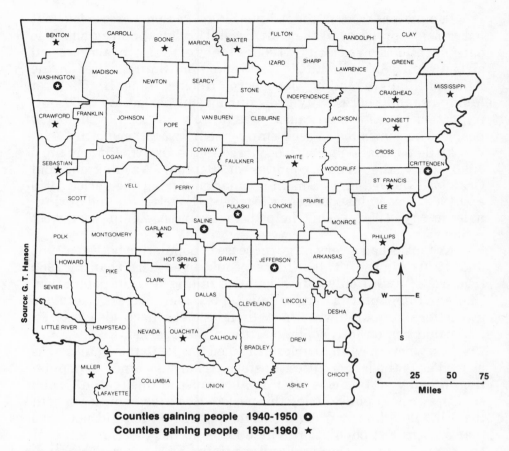

Counties gaining people 1940-1950 ⊙
Counties gaining people 1950-1960 ★

Figure 35. Population changes, 1940-1960.

The Ouachita region also lost population during the 1940 to 1960 period. Especially hard hit were the southern counties of the region and counties in the Arkansas River Valley. Farming was more important in this region than elsewhere. Yet these counties also lost population. A few counties in the Ouachitas did gain population. These were counties with large cities like Little Rock, Fort Smith, and Hot Springs. As in the 1940's and 1950's, the cities grew by attracting people from the rural areas. Undoubtedly, some of the rural losses in the other counties of the region were people who moved to these cities.

Population losses in the Alluvial Plain region were serious but not as widespread as in the Gulf Coastal or Ouachita regions. The out-migration slowed a bit by 1950 as many of the farm laborers had already left. As with Little Rock and Fort Smith, cities in the Alluvial Plain including Jonesboro, Helena, Pine Bluff, West Memphis, and Forrest City grew during this period. By 1960, out-migration in eastern Arkansas was largely confined to the black people who continued to seek employment in northern cities.

Little population growth occurred in the Ozarks Plateau until 1960. Only the urban counties of Benton, Washington, and Crawford showed any gains in population during the period 1940 and 1960. New industries began to move to Fayetteville and Springdale in the 1950's. This helped to keep people in northwest Arkansas.

Arkansas had a very large increase in population between 1960 and 1970. Almost 137,000 more people lived here than in 1960 (Figure 36), with only a few counties failing to gain population. The environmental factors of hills, lakes, and rivers were major attractions. Small town life with its slower pace also was an important reason for people to settle in the Ozarks.

Elsewhere new industries attracted people to the small towns as well as to the larger cities. Eastern Arkansas gained in population in many of its towns after 1960 because of this reason. Urban counties grew rapidly during this period. However, counties in both the Alluvial Plain and Gulf Coastal regions which did not have many towns lost population. These losses in the 1960's meant that the rural **depopulation** was still continuing.

Future Population Change

Arkansas' future is one of continued population growth. Arkansas is one of the **Sun Belt** states. The mild climate and environmental factors of the Sun Belt attract people and businesses alike. These attractions, which Arkansas possesses, continue to draw industries from northern states. The attraction also brings more people who retire to live in Arkansas. The 1980 Census showed that Arkansas' population is now 2,279,417. Experts predict the state's population to continue its increase during the decade of the 1980's. By 1990, the northwest part of Arkansas will have over 13 percent of the state's population. We can expect the

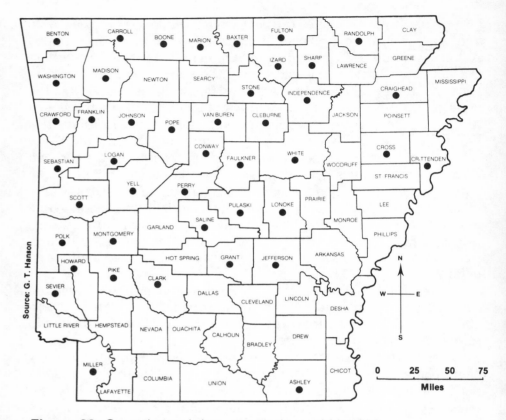

Figure 36. Counties gaining population, 1960-1970.

Ozarks and to a lesser degree, the Ouachitas, to increase in population more rapidly in the future. Eastern Arkansas, however, is expected to lose population through the next ten years.

Agriculture continues to be important in eastern Arkansas. We can expect the rural out-migration to slow down in the future here. In addition, new industries are coming to many of the small towns in this region. These industries are offering jobs and will attract people to them. The rural to urban movement from Arkansas to northern cities has probably stopped and is unlikely to start up again. It appears, then, that our state's serious loss of population which we saw in the 1940 to 1960 period is over. In the future we can look forward to population growth, some of which will be significant in selected areas.

Key Words and Activities

Key Words

Population change	Out-migration
Rural to urban migration	In-migration
Depopulation	

Student Activities

1. Which of the areas of Arkansas had large populations before 1940?
2. What reasons can you give for population losses in Arkansas before 1940?
3. Why did rural areas lose more people than urban areas between 1900 and 1960?
4. Locate your county on a map. What happened to population in your county from 1900 to 1940? From 1940 to 1960, did your county gain or lose population?
5. What reasons can you list that caused these losses or gains?
6. What two reasons can you give for the large increases in the state's population after 1960?
7. Name five important cities in Arkansas which grew rapidly after 1960.

Selected References

Industrial Research and Extension Center. *Arkansas Population Projections 1970-1990 By Planning and Development District*. Little Rock: College of Business Administration, 1973.

U.S. Department of Commerce. *Census Reports*. Washington D.C.: Bureau of the Census, 1900-1970.

U.S. Department of Commerce. *Population Estimates*. Bureau of the Census, Washington D.C., various years.

Chapter 12

LAND USE IN ARKANSAS

A major interest we have in our state is what uses are made of our land. Land uses across Arkansas are varied because of the different physical features and the different people who live here. When we talk about land use, we refer to what sort of activities take place on the land. There are many types of land use.

For example, farming is one use for land. Mining, forestry, and recreational land uses also are found in Arkansas. The land our homes occupy is **residential land**. Schools such as the one you go to are part of **public land**. Our highways and railroads take up a large portion of land and are part of the **transportation land use** in the state.

Before we look at land uses in detail, let us talk about the types of uses we put our land to in Arkansas. In a recent survey of the land of our state it was found that two categories of land uses covered most of the state. **Forest land** and **agricultural land uses** made up more than 92 percent of all of the land. Wetlands occupy 2.6 percent and water bodies cover only 2.5 percent of Arkansas' total land area. Cities and towns occupy only 2 percent of the total acreage in Arkansas. You can see then that most of the land in our state is devoted to either forests or farming in the state. Let us look closer at these categories of land use and find out what kinds of activities occur there.

Forest lands are not all used for lumber production. Some of the forest land does have timber cutting activities going on, but other forest land may be left alone. In Arkansas, a great many acres of trees are in national forests. Some of these national forests have recreational areas within them. Camping, hiking, and picnicking activities occur in these recreational areas. So other uses are made of the forest lands besides timber production.

Agriculture is concentrated in the Alluvial Plain and Arkansas River Valley counties. In these two regions, a majority of the land is in farms. As you might expect, most of the land is either used for crops such as rice, soybeans, and cotton. Hay also is grown on the farmlands across the Arkansas River Valley. Little farming occurs in the Ouachita or Ozarks natural region and the percent of farm land in these two regions is very small.

Another type of land use in Arkansas is for urban activities. **Urban land** use includes all land used for homes, apartment buildings, and mobile homes. **Industrial** land is included in this category. Also we add transportation facilities to the urban land use. This includes roads, railroads, streets, and airports. Finally, stores and businesses are part of the urban land use.

When we look at all of the land in Arkansas, not much of it goes for urban land use. One of the reasons for this is that most cities and towns are compact and are not spread out over the countryside. Within our urban places, about one-third of the urban land is for residential use. Another important use of urban land is for the factories and industrial plants found in many of our cities.

Many times land has multiple uses. This often leads to competition for land. For example, if forest land is to be used for recreation, lumber cutting would not be possible because it would compete with the recreatioal activities. If the land is used for farming, we would not expect to build houses or roads on these agricultural plots. Competition for land is a serious problem for many areas in Arkansas. If we are to make the best possible use of our land, we must learn what the land is being used for today.

We will examine several types of land uses in Arkansas in the next few chapters. Farming is one of our most important uses of land. Forestry and mining activities also occur in many counties of Arkansas. These are important to our economy and to the people of the state. Industrial land use, while it is confined mostly to the cities, is also examined for its meaning to the state's land uses. Finally, we will examine recreational land uses and what they mean to our people and to tourists.

Key Words and Activities

Key Words

Land use	Agricultural land use
Residential land use	Mining land use
Industrial land use	Forest land use
Transportational land use	Urban land use
Public land use	

Student Activities

1. What are some land uses which can be found in your town or county?
2. What different land uses would occur in towns from those uses found in the rural areas of your county?
3. Give three examples of public land uses in your town or county.

Selected References

Land Use Maps, *Atlas of Arkansas*, Little Rock, Arkansas: Department of Planning, 1973.

Topographic Quadrangle Maps, Arkansas Geological Commission, Little Rock, Arkansas.

Chapter 13

AGRICULTURE IN ARKANSAS

Farming is one of the state's most important economic activities. Just as there are many different physical regions in Arkansas, there are also many types of farming across our state.

As we look at farming differences in Arkansas, we must remember that many factors work together to produce crops and animals. Physical features such as climate, soils, vegetation, water, and terrain are important influences in farming. The flatter the land, the easier it becomes to farm, but adequate drainage of this land is a critical factor in parts of Arkansas.

There are also many aspects of man and his technology which affect farming. In parts of our state farmers rely heavily upon machines to do the work. The demand for Arkansas' crops in distant states and even foreign countries makes for changes in farming. We will examine each of the six natural regions of Arkansas and learn what farming is like in each region.

Four major types of farming are found in Arkansas. These are **commercial cash crop farming, livestock raising, special fruit and vegetable farming,** and **general farming.** Commercial cash crop farming is a situation in which a farmer grows crops to sell outside of Arkansas. The chief crops raised are cotton, rice, and soybeans. Commercial farming usually requires large tractors and other machinery to do the work. Livestock raising is a type of farming which produces only animals. Most livestock farmers have either cattle or poultry. Fruit and vegetable farming is limited to only a few areas in the state. This type of farming has many different crops such as grapes, peaches, pears and apples. Vegetables such as tomatoes and beans are also included in this type of farming. Finally, general farming is also found throughout the state. A great variety of crops and animals are raised on these farms. Most of the crops and animals on general farms, however, are not sold beyond the state.

Farms in Arkansas have shown several trends since 1850 (Table 4). The total number of farms rose from 1850 to 1930. During the same period, average farm size decreased. More farms caused a decline in the average size. After 1930, however, the number of farms dropped sharply until 1969. Notice what happened to farm size during this period. It rises with the loss of farms. By 1969, the average farm in Arkansas was 260 acres.

TABLE 4
Arkansas Farm Changes, 1850 to 1969

Year	Average Farm Size (acres)	Number of Farms
1850	146	18,000
1860	245	39,000
1870	154	49,000
1880	128	94,000
1890	119	125,000
1900	93	179,000
1910	81	215,000
1920	75	233,000
1930	66	242,000
1940	83	217,000
1950	103	182,000
1960	173	95,000
1969	260	60,000

SOURCE: *Historical Statistics of the United States*, 1978.

Alluvial Plain Farming

The richest soils and largest farms are found in the Alluvial Plain region (Figure 37). Farms here often cover several hundred acres. Most farms are owned and operated by the families who live on the farm. Planting and harvesting is done mainly by machines. A typical farm here might include two tractors, a combine, cultivator discs, and two or three planters. One of the reasons for the great numbers of machines is the rich, level land found in this area. Do you remember what the region looks like? Most of the area is very flat and has thick layers of stream deposited material. The flatness of the land makes it easy to use machines. The rich soil helps farmers produce a wide variety of crops. Farmland in these counties also receives ample rainfall plus available underground water. The underground water is used to irrigate crops like rice and cotton. A long growing season permits crops to mature and produce large yields.

Since 1900, farm size has increased in the region. Farms have grown larger because more swamp land has been drained. Also, forests have been cleared so crops can be grown.

Many other small farms which were marginal or not profitable to operate have been sold to larger farmers. With the coming of larger farms, more machines are required to do the work. As more machines are used, more land can be put into crops.

Farmers in eastern Arkansas grow large amounts of cotton, soybeans, and rice. In the past, cotton was the major crop. Since 1950, however, rice has become much more important. Recently, a new crop—soybeans—has been raised on the Alluvial Plain with great success. Because soybeans grow well in most types of soils and water conditions, they have been planted on old cotton fields and on newly drained lands.

Cotton is a highly mechanized crop. The field preparation, planting, and early cultivation are all done by large tractors and equipment. In addition, crop-dusting airplanes are used to apply fertilizers and chemicals to kill weeds and harmful insects. The harvesting of cotton is also done by machine. The large cotton pickers which move through the fields in the fall are another example of the cotton farmer's dependence upon machines. The leading cotton producing counties in 1977 were Mississippi, Jeffer-

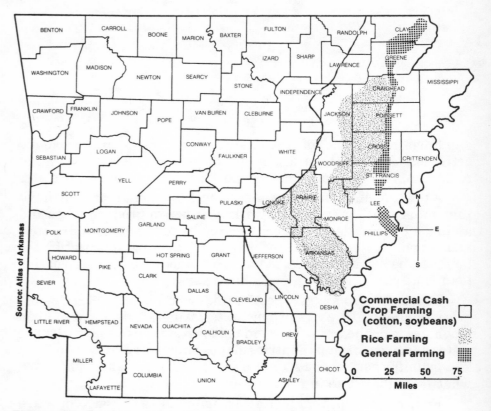

Figure 37. Eastern Arkansas farming regions.

son, and Craighead. Almost one fifth of the cultivated land in these counties went to cotton. Cotton is important in Poinsett, Lee, Crittenden, Desha, Lincoln, Ashley, and Phillips Counties. All other counties in the region raise some cotton but it is not the most important crop.

Rice farming is limited to certain areas in the Alluvial Plain. Growing rice requires level land, great amounts of water, and levees built around the fields. Rice is often planted and fertilized by crop-dusting airplanes. If you look at the map of farming in eastern Arkansas, you can find two areas of rice farming (Figure 37). Lonoke, Arkansas, and Prairie Counties are the heart of the rice country. A second group of rice-producing counties exists west of Crowley's Ridge.

Soybean production in Arkansas has increased very rapidly since 1960. It has become the most important crop in eastern Arkansas, replacing cotton and rice. More acres are planted in soybeans than in any other crop.

One reason for the crop's importance is the great demand for soybeans. They are used in many food products and as a source of protein in the United States. Many foreign countries also buy this crop. Soybeans are used in cooking oil, baby food, meat substitutes, and cereals. Many of the products we buy in the grocery store are made with soybeans. Soybeans are easily planted on almost any type of land. If the soils are moderately rich and the land is level, the crop does very well. Mississippi County leads all others in soybean production. Crittenden, Phillips, Arkansas, Poinsett, Jackson, Cross, and Jefferson Counties also have large acreages devoted to soybeans. We can expect soybeans to continue as a major crop in eastern Arkansas for many years to come.

Farming on Crowley's Ridge

Crowley's Ridge is that narrow band of hills stretching north and south across the Alluvial Plain from the Missouri border to Helena, Arkansas (Figure 37). The ridge, made up of the fine silt or loess which is wind-deposited, is an area elevated above the Alluvial Plain. Farming on the Ridge is more difficult than on the Alluvial Plain because of the more steeply sloping land and the more easily eroded soil. Soil erosion is actually a significant problem for Ridge farmers. Farmers use fewer machines and farms are smaller than on the Alluvial Plain.

General farming and cotton production began on the ridge in the 1880's. Small farms raised a considerable variety of crops and animals. Today, cotton production is declining in the area. In its place, cattle raising and dairy production are becoming commonplace. Cotton production has decreased as it is easier and more profitable to raise cotton on the Alluvial Plain. Farmers found a greater demand for meat and dairy products than for cotton, so they have shifted to raising beef cattle and dairy cows. Often these farmers do not raise any crops on their land. Elsewhere on Crowley's Ridge general farming occurs.

Gulf Coastal Plain Farming

Farming in the Gulf Coastal Plain is not as widespread or as prosperous as in eastern Arkansas. Since people first moved into the region, farming has always been on a small scale. The average farm is less than 200 acres in most counties in the region and the value of an acre of land is among the lowest in the state. Farms are also less productive here than in eastern Arkansas primarily because of environmental conditions.

A major factor limiting agriculture is the extremely poor soil. Much of the region has infertile soils called red-yellow podzols. These soils are poorly suited for crop production but do support pine trees and grasses suited for pasture. Despite a long growing season and ample rainfall, crops like cotton, rice, and soybeans do not grow well in the thin, unproductive soils. The only areas of rich soils exist in the narrow river bottoms of the Red, Ouachita, and Saline Rivers. One problem with these lands, however, is that they flood.

Despite these limitations on farming, many agricultural activities do exist in the Coastal Plain. Perhaps the most important farming involves livestock raising. Much of the land here is too poor for crop farming. Raising cattle and poultry are more profitable forms of farming (Figure 38). Cattle raising is more widespread than in eastern Arkansas. Leading counties for cattle production are in the southwest corner of the region. Hay, which is used for cattle food, is also an important farming product. Many of the same counties important for cattle production are also centers for poultry raising. Less land is needed for raising chickens and turkeys than for cattle. A poultry farm is easily recognized by the long, low buildings which house the poultry. The chickens and turkeys raised in this region are sold to food processing plants and supermarkets all across the United States. Limited crop production does occur in the Gulf Coastal Plains. Counties along the Red River are the largest soybean and rice producers in the region.

Farming in the Ouachita Mountain Region

Farming occurs in this region only in scattered locations. Traditionally, this area has had few people and isolated farms. This trend has continued to the present as we find only about 4,300 farms

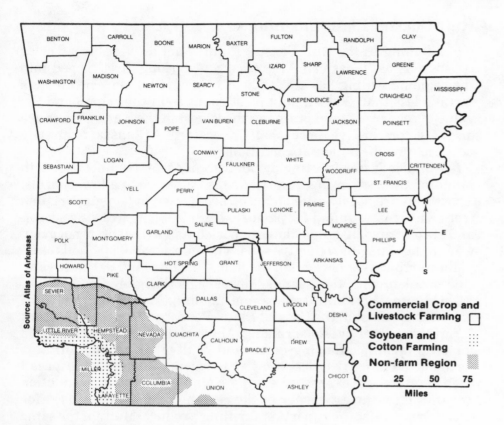

Figure 38. Gulf Coastal Plains farming.

Hay is the most important crop grown in the region and is sold for animal food in Arkansas, Texas, and Oklahoma. Hay can be grown on infertile soils and does not need a long growing season or temperatures.

Arkansas River Valley Farming

The broad bottomlands between the Ozark Mountains and the Ouachitas is one of the more important farming areas in Arkansas. The deep, rich soils, level land, ample rainfall, and the long growing season all favor farming. These environmental conditions make farming more profitable here than in the Gulf Coastal Plain or the Ouachitas.

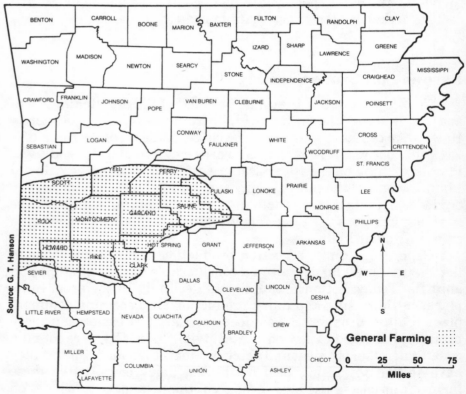

Figure 39. Ouachita Region farming.

scattered over eight counties (Figure 39). The farm size is extremely small in most counties. The largest farms are in Yell County, which has an average farm size of 219 acres. This average is several acres below the state average farm size.

Landforms of the Ouachitas play an important role in determining where farms are located. The land has steep slopes which are covered with thin, acid soils and pine forests. In addition, the growing season is shorter here than in the Alluvial Plain or the Coastal Plain. These environmental conditions make crop farming difficult. It is easier to use the land for timber growing or to clear only a small amount of land for pasture or crops.

General farming is the major agricultural activity in this area.

Farming began in the early 1800's in the Valley. Farms were generally larger than in areas south or north of the River Valley. This pattern of larger farms continues today. While some livestock raising exists in the Valley, crop farming is the most important agricultural activity.

Soybeans have become the major crop (Figure 40). This crop has replaced cotton, which was once raised in every county in the Valley. Important soybean counties include Crawford, Conway, Faulkner, and Perry. Cotton is important today only in Conway County. Another crop, rice, is raised in Perry and Faulkner Counties, although only 3,000 acres were grown in 1976.

The hilly portions of the Arkansas River Valley support scattered general farms. Livestock raising is the most common activity on many of these farms. Little crop farming occurs in the hills due to the steep slopes and thin, infertile soils.

Farming in the Ozarks

The physical environment of the Ozarks makes farming difficult. Much of the land is in steep slopes. Rocky, thin soils which are not very fertile hamper the growing of crops and the raising of livestock. The rocky soils are easily washed away unless a vegetation cover is present. Erosion is a serious problem here. Much of the land is covered by a thick oak-hickory forest with little land cleared for crops or pasture. Only in northwest Arkansas in Benton and Washington Counties has there been any extensive clearing for farming. The growing season in the Ozarks is also shorter than anywhere else in the state. Here the last killing frost in spring occurs in late April while the first killing frost occurs in late October.

Most of the farms in the Ozarks are small and family-owned and operated. Farmers in the Ozarks rely less heavily upon machines than do farmers in eastern Arkansas and are not as productive.

General farming and livestock raising are the two most important types of farming in the Ozarks. The general farm here, like others in the state, contains a variety of crops and animals. Livestock raising has become more important in recent years. Beef cattle and dairy herds are especially numerous in northwest Arkansas (Figure 41). Poultry raising is concentrated in Washington, Benton, Carroll, and Madison Counties. Poultry farms do not need very much cleared space and can be started on the smallest of farms. Northwest Arkansas is one of the state's most important fruit and vegetable growing areas. Apple production is concentrated in Washington, Benton, and Carroll Counties. Other crops such as snap beans, spinach, tomatoes, and peaches are found in these counties as well as in Madison, Boone, and Marion Counties.

Agriculture continues to be one of Arkansas' most important activities. Many thousands of people work on farms and help to supply the farmers with needed products. Production of crops and animals will continue to be necessary to our state as long as people

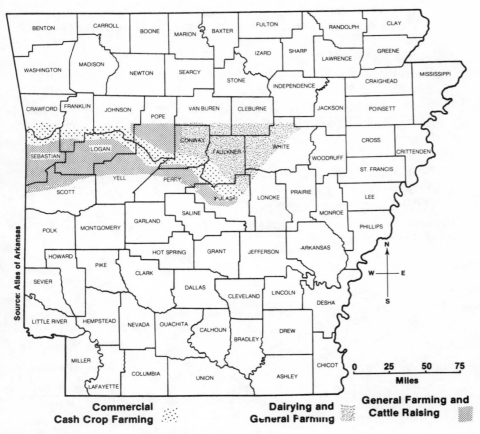

Figure 40. Arkansas River Valley farming.

live here. Because of this, it is necessary to protect our soil and water resources. Protection against soil erosion and water shortages will enable farmers to continue to grow crops and raise animals. In order to protect our soil and water resources, we must understand what types of uses occur on our land.

Key Words and Activities

Key Words

Agriculture

Commercial crop farming

Livestock raising

Fruit and vegetable farming

General farming

Student Activities

1. List the major environmental factors which affect farming for each of the six natural regions.
2. Which counties in the Gulf Coastal Plains and the Ozarks are important areas for poultry production?
3. In which region is cotton the most important crop? Why is it so important here?
4. Which counties specialize in rice production in Arkansas?

Selected References

Agriculture Maps, *Atlas of Arkansas*. Little Rock: Department of Planning, 1973.

U. S. Department of Agriculture, *Agricultural Statistics for Arkansas*. Little Rock: Economics, Statistics, and Cooperatives Service, 1970-Present.

U. S. Department of Agriculture. *Crop and Livestock Reports*. Little Rock: Economics, Statistics, and Cooperative Service, Monthly.

U. S. Department of Agriculture. *Yearbook of Agriculture*. Washington, D.C.: Government Printing Office, various years.

University of Arkansas. *Arkansas Crop Production*. Fayetteville: Division of Agriculture, 1979.

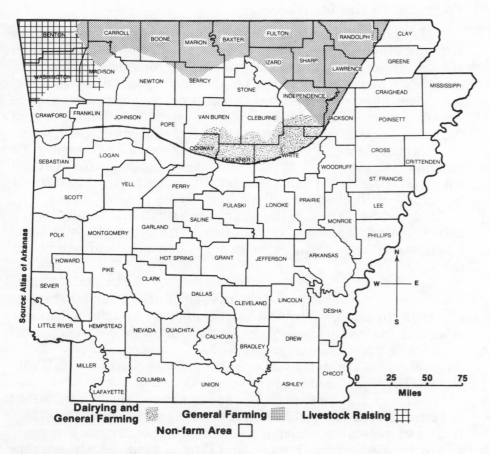

Dairying and General Farming   General Farming   Livestock Raising   Non-farm Area

Figure 41. Ozark Mountain farming.

Chapter 14

FOREST LAND USE

The forests have been among man's oldest allies, providing food, shelter, building materials, firewood, and even clothing. Man may have first managed to live in communities on forest margins and even today the forests of the world provide important resources for human use. Building materials, paper, plywood, and several other kinds of specialized woods come from forests. It is not surprising that the earth today no longer carries the forest cover it once did. It is estimated that about half the earth's land area was covered with forests when man's exploitation began, and today the figure is down to approximately 25 percent. Some areas have been completely cleared or very nearly so. China is such an area, and the Mediterranean and Western Europe are also largely deforested. The next time you drive through the Arkansas Valley or across eastern Arkansas, look around you and imagine that, not very long ago, your path would have led through mile after mile of forest.

Even though forest land has been on the decline in many states and even in Arkansas, it is by far the most extensive land use in our state. Fortunately, forests are renewable resources, even with intensive harvesting, if managed properly. This renewable resource, requiring from 30 to 200 years to regenerate, has many important functions besides providing firewood, paper products, and building materials.

According to some, "Trees are the great healers of nature." Forests absorb, hold, and release water, preserve the soil and life systems for entire regions, and they affect the climate by producing oxygen and absorbing heat. Moreover, they provide habitat for plant and animal life, help absorb some air pollutants and noise, and serve as a source of beauty and esthetic pleasure to relieve the monotony of man's cultural landscape.

Current Acreage and Ownership

Forestry, the greatest land use in Arkansas, occupies 17.2 million acres or 51 percent of the state's total land area. Other major uses of land include farmland and pasture, and urban and miscellaneous uses.

Major changes are occurring in the amount of forest resources available in our state as is illustrated by the constant and rather widespread decline in acreage devoted to forest. Land in forest declined by 12 percent from 1959 to 1969 and by 4 percent from 1969 to 1979. Only 19 counties have more forest land today than in 1969. Much of the forest land is being cleared for cropland and pasture. Smaller amounts are being converted to urban uses. Hardwood forests have experienced the most significant reductions, especially within the Mississippi Alluvial Plain. The decline in the Alluvial Plain was no surprise since farms had been displacing prime hardwood timber there for many years. The decline of the 1960's was a period of even more rapid clearing on the Alluvial Plain as soybeans became more and more popular.

Ownership of the forest lands is not dominated by any particular group. Farmers control approximately 26 percent and the forest industry owns 22 percent. Private non-industrial owners hold slightly over 35 percent of the forests. The remaining 16 to 17 percent is in public ownership, most of which is in national forests.

Approximately 3 million acres of timberland are included within the two national forests in Arkansas. The U. S. Forest Service has developed campgrounds at scenic points in these woodlands. The largest of the two is the 1,576,870-acre Ouachita National Forest in the Ouachita Mountains Province. Second in size is the Ozark-St. Francis National Forest with 1,135,087 acres located primarily in the Boston Mountains. The small St. Francis segment is the only national forest land in eastern Arkansas. Trees within these national forests are available for selective and controlled harvesting. These forests are also used for recreation, watershed preservation, and environmental protection.

Arkansas' volume of growing stock on commercial forest land exceeded 15 billion cubic feet in 1970. Approximately 57 percent of this growing stock inventory was hardwood and 43 percent pine. The total volume of saw-timber of more than 46 billion board feet in 1970 was 55 percent pine and 45 percent hardwood.

Distribution of Forest Land

The Arkansas Forestry Commission, for purposes of data collection and regional comparison, has divided the state into four survey regions including the **1. Delta, 2. Southwest, 3. Ouachita,** and **4. Ozark Survey Region.** The location of these four survey regions is presented in Figure 42.

Forest land in Arkansas is not evenly distributed. Forest are actually strongly concentrated in the western one-half of the state (Table 5). The **Southwest Survey Region** alone contains one-third (more than 6.4 million acres) of the state's forested areas and almost half of the total timber volume. This region has also lost less land to other uses in the past decade than any other region, less than 5 percent. Almost half of the timberland is owned by forest industries. Ten of 19 counties with at least 75 percent of their land area in forest are located in the Southwest, which further illustrates the extensiveness of forests in this region.

Forests are also quite extensive in the **Ozark Survey Region,** where approximately 6.0 million acres are found. Forests occupy 60 percent of the total land area. As is obvious from Table 5, the Alluvial Plain **(Delta Survey Region)** has been extensively cleared and now has only 1.7 million acres of forest. Only 10.6 percent of its total land area is now devoted to forests that are widely scattered and not economically feasible for marketing. Extensive drainage and clearing of these flood plain lands have substantially increased farmland acreage and have resulted in the drastic reduction of bottomland hardwood forests in eastern Arkansas. The **Ouachita Region,** with its 3.0 million acres in forest, seems relatively insignificant when compared with the Southwest or the Ozarks, yet 70 percent of its total land area is in forest uses. The total acreage in

Figure 42. Forest survey regions in Arkansas.

TABLE 5
Commercial Forest Land In Arkansas, 1970

Survey Region	Commercial Forest (thousand acres)	Change Since Last Survey (percent)	Proportion of Region Forested[1] (percent)
Delta	1,725.0	-39	11
Southwest	6,415.1	-5	75
Ouachita	3,069.1	-7	70
Ozark	6,017.5	-10	60
All Regions	17,226.7	-12	51

[1]Total forest including noncommercial as a proportion of total area in the region.

forest figures is relatively small because the overall size of the region is small. This region has almost half of the forest land in public ownership, mainly the Ouachita National Forest. Shortleaf pine is the most valuable commercial species on much of the area. The region also has a recreational potential that is probably as high as it is for timber production.

Three major forest types stand out in distinct patterns across Arkansas. The Alluvial Plain of eastern Arkansas is an area dominated by **Bottomland Hardwood** with sizable acreages of prairie and areas where forests are extremely limited. The Ozarks of northern Arkansas and the Arkansas Valley have two major forest types. **Upland Hardwoods** are the most extensive with relatively large areas of the **Loblolly Pine-Hardwood type.** The Ouachita Mountains and the West Gulf Coastal Plain are dominated by **Loblolly-Shortleaf Pine** interspersed with a few hardwood trees. Pine types form broad and extensive patterns across several counties in western and southern Arkansas and often occupy 80 to 90 percent of the total land area (Figure 15, Chapter 5, p. 19). Forestry and forest-related activities are vital to local economies of these regions and losses to farming activities that are so pronounced in eastern Arkansas have not occurred in western and southern Arkansas. Here forest land remains as a dominant feature of the physical landscape.

Marketing, Employment, and Manufacturing

Approximately 569 million cubic feet of products were harvested from Arkansas forests in 1978. The mainstays of the timber economy are saw logs and pulpwood. The pulp industry increased its capacity by 40 percent from 1968 to 1978, and Arkansas has pioneered in southern pine plywood production.

Almost 70 percent of Arkansas' 1978 timber harvest was made into saw logs. Two-thirds of the 1.2 billion board feet of logs were softwood species, nearly all pine. Oak supplied 57 percent of the hardwood used.

The wood and wood products industry is one of the largest industries in the state. The largest wood related corporations include Georgia-Pacific, International Paper, and Weyerhauser. Georgia-Pacific has plants in Crossett, Fordyce, Stamps, El Dorado, and Glenwood and ranks second among Arkansas industries in the number of employees with a total exceeding 4,400. International Paper has factories in Benton, Bierne, Delight, Gurdon, Leola, Pine Bluff, Rison, and Russellville and with its 3,800 employees ranks third in the number of persons employed. Weyerhauser has plants in Mountain Pine, De Queen, Pine Bluff, Dierks, Brier (Nashville), and West Memphis and employs 2,776 people. Approximately 25 percent of all manufacturing employment is timber-related. In 1970, a total of 42,027 people were employed in wood manufacturing with over 50 percent of these working in timber and wood products.

The wood-manufacturing payrolls exceeded $242,900,000 for employees in 1970 with 43 percent of the wages being earned in the lumbering and wood products segment.

Timber supplied raw material for more than 600 wood manufacturing plants within the state. Almost every county has a primary wood-using industry, usually a sawmill. Pulpwood consumption by Arkansas mills has increased by almost one-half since 1968. Arkansas' veneer industry has also increased in recent years in the state.

In addition to the manufacturing facilities already described, Arkansas has approximately 40 other primary wood-using plants. The plants make coops, handles, and veneers, while others are involved in wood preserving, charcoal production, and some 30 to 40 miscellaneous activities.

Summary

As can be seen from the preceding discussion, Arkansas has varied and extensive forest cover. How should these vast forest resources best be used? Some suggest a management system similar to the one applied to our national forests. National forests are managed under the **Multiple Use Sustained Yield Act of 1960** and the **1974 and 1976 Forest Reserves Management Acts.** These acts are based on the principle of multiple use that is balanced among the following purposes: (1) timbering, (2) watershed maintenance, (3) wildlife habitat preservation, and (4) recreation. Short-term economical benefits to be gained from timber products should be balanced with long-range protection of soil, the watershed, wildlife, and scenery and with assurances that areas will be replanted for future needs with no one use becoming dominant.

Since forests require from 30 to 200 years for regrowth, much care and consideration should be given to forest management practices. Forests are usually harvested by either **selective cutting** or **clear-cutting.** In selective cutting, or thinning, individual mature trees scattered throughout a stand are cut, while young trees are left to grow to maturity. This uneven-age method is particularly useful in forests with trees of different species and ages, and it does not significantly alter the natural appearance of such forests. It is the method favored by those wishing to use forests for various purposes and those wishing to preserve mature forests.

Clear-cutting means removing all trees from an area. When done properly, the resulting debris and litter are removed or burned, and the area is reseeded so that a new crop of trees, all the same age, can be clear-cut decades later. This method creates a checkerboard of patches, each patch comprising trees of the same age.

Clear-cutting is a controversial form of forest management. The timber companies favor clear-cutting because it is relatively quick, and it saves money since the cutting activities occupy a limited area, thus reducing the number of logging roads needed at any one time. Also, clear-cut forests grow back faster because the seedlings get more sunlight than in selectively cut forests, a fact that enables more frequent harvesting.

Negative aspects of clear-cutting are: (1) it creates ugly scars that take years to heal, (2) it replaces a diverse stand of trees with an even-aged stand that is more susceptible to insects, disease, wind, and fire, (3) clear-cutting can destroy wildlife habitats, (4) it causes extensive soil erosion and depletes soil nutrients, and (5) it lowers water tables and reduces water quality.

Some argue that large-scale clear-cutting violates the multiple use concept of forest management by degrading soil and water quality and by making national forests unsuitable for recreation. Fortunately, Congress has eased the controversy by passing the **National Forest Management Act of 1976.** This law allows some clear-cutting in national forests but only under strictly controlled conditions and after trees have reached a minimum age.

This **multiple use** practice is suggested for Arkansas' vast forest resources. Even though our forests are quite extensive and appear to be abundant, wise management designed to allow for the greatest use and benefit and at the same time provide a sustained yield of forestry products is the most desirable.

Key Words and Activities

Key Words

Forest survey region	Selective cutting
Multiple use concept	Clear cutting

Student Activities

1. What major types of forests and product activities occur in your county or town?
2. What is meant by the multiple use idea of forest management?
3. What are some representative types of forest product industries which are found in Arkansas?

Selected References

Arkansas Forestry Commission. *Forestry: Its Economic and Environmental Importance to Arkansas.* Little Rock, Arkansas, 1972.

U. S. Department of Agriculture, Forest Service, *Arkansas Forest Resources Patterns.* Southern Forest Experiment Station, Resources Bulletin SO-24, New Orleans, Louisiana, 1970.

U. S. Department of Agriculture, Forest Service. *Arkansas Forest,* Herbert S. Steinitzke. Southern Forest Experiment Station, New Orleans, Louisiana, 1960.

U. S. Department of Agriculture, Forest Service. *Forest Statistics For Arkansas Counties,* by Arnold Hedlund and J. M. Earles. U. S. Forest Service Resource Bulletin SO-22, Southern Forest Experiment Station, New Orleans, Louisiana, 1970.

Chapter 15

MINING IN ARKANSAS

Arkansas has many minerals within its boundaries. Several of these minerals are currently being mined, and others mined in the past are no longer being extracted. There are three types of mining in Arkansas: **open pit, strip and shaft or underground mining**. All three types differ in the method used to take the minerals out of the ground.

Open pit mining is easily recognized by the very large and often deep hole in the ground. The open pit method is used in Arkansas to mine bauxite. Open pit mines usually are worked for many years. The soil and other unusable rock materials are scraped away and piled alongside the open pit. Mining then begins, and the pit gets wider as more minerals are taken out of the mine. Large machines load the minerals onto trucks or railcars and minerals are carried to the plant where they are turned into metals.

Strip mining is quite different from open pit mining. The strip mine is rarely more than a few feet deep and often covers only a small amount of ground. One of the minerals which is strip mined in Arkansas is coal. The soil is stripped away along with the loose rock. Once the coal is mined and the supply is exhausted, the soils and loose rock are put back into place. The land is usually restored to its original contour before it was stripped. This is called **reclamation of the land**.

A third type of mining, **shaft or underground mining**, is found less frequently in the state. This type of mining is done underground. All that one could see on the surface is the shaft. Small amounts of coal are mined this way in Arkansas. Oil and natural gas recovery, a type of mining, involves underground drilling and the extraction of petroleum and natural gas from wells at varying depths below the ground.

Mineral Resources of Arkansas

Coal is a mineral resource which is made up of decayed vegetation. Dead vegetation piles up over millions of years and is slowly compressed into rock. There are three types of coal in Arkansas: **semi-anthracite, bituminous** or soft coal, and **lignite**. Most of the coal mined today is either semi-anthracite or bituminous coal. Lignite, however, may become very important in the future.

The semi-anthracite coal is used to help make iron and steel in factories in Illinois and Ohio. Most of this coal is used for smelters in these states and very little of the semi-anthracite coal is used in Arkansas.

Arkansas bituminous coal is used chiefly for thermal electric generating plants. These plants burn coal to heat water and to make steam. The steam is used to turn huge turbines which produce electricity. Since only a few Arkansas power plants use bituminous coal, most of it is shipped out of the state. It is likely that more bituminous coal will be used in the future for electricity production as oil and natural gas supplies decrease.

Arkansas' major coalfield is located in the western Arkansas River Valley (Figure 43). The field is about thirty-three miles wide and sixty miles long and covers a portion of Sebastian, Franklin, Johnson, and Logan Counties. The earliest coal mining in the 1870's was shaft mining. Several railroads were built to the mines between 1870 and 1888 to haul the coal to the markets. In 1907, more than 2.75 million tons of coal were mined. Since then, however, production has declined. Although shaft mining was used in the past, today most coal is mined by the strip mine method.

Lignite deposits are concentrated in the south central sections of the Gulf Coastal Plain. This mineral is a form of coal which is very soft and light brown in color. Lignite does not burn as well as bituminous or semi-anthracite coals. It has been used for heating, as a

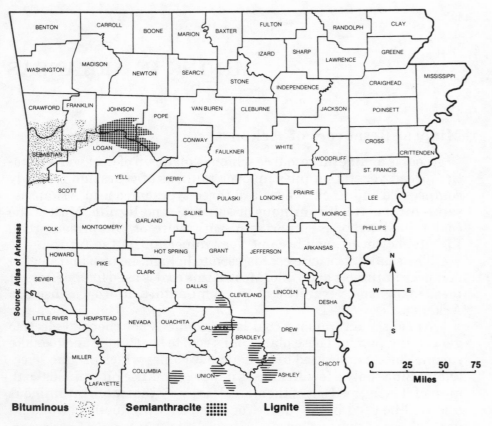

Figure 43. Coal and lignite deposits.

although it did not produce at its maximum for very long. From this early beginning, Arkansas oil and gas exploration spread across the state in Union, Columbia, Lafayette, and Miller Counties. Natural gas fields also were discovered in the western part of the Arkansas River Valley.

Since 1945, oil production has remained about the same from year to year with only slight changes. With a growing demand for petroleum, we can expect more exploration and production of oil in Arkansas. Natural gas production increased between 1920 and 1945 then fell in the 1950's. Since then, however, production has risen each year.

source of dye, and as a wax in the past. Although lignite has been mined in scattered locations in the state in the past, it has not been very important. However, lignite will probably be used in some electric plants in the future. If this occurs, Arkansas lignite will be strip mined.

Arkansas has moderate amounts of petroleum and natural gas (Figure 44). While the fields are smaller than those in Louisiana, Texas, or Oklahoma, the state's oil resources are important to its economy. The earliest gas field was brought into production in the Fort Smith area in 1900. The real oil boom began in 1921 in Union County with the first big oil well coming in near Smackover. The Smackover field became the largest and the richest in the state

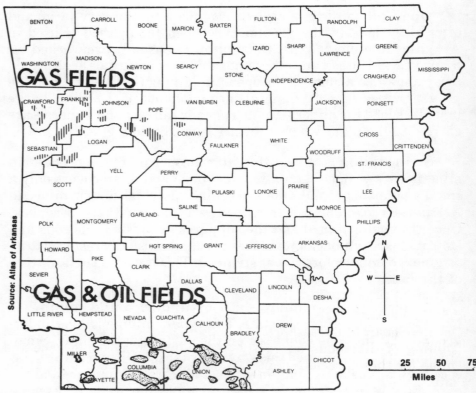

Figure 44. Gas and oil fields.

Bauxite production in the state began in the late 1880's. Bauxite is used to make aluminum products. It was first discovered in Saline County, and later deposits were located in nearby Pulaski County. These are the only two counties where this mineral is found. The bauxite is taken out of the ground primarily by the open pit method of mining. Since 1900, Arkansas has led all other states in bauxite production. It has produced almost 95 percent of the country's bauxite. Currently, bauxite is the principal mineral ore being mined in the state. Three companies mine bauxite in our state: Reynold's Mining Corporation, Alcoa, and American Cyanamid Company. There are two major processing plants which turn bauxite into aluminum metal. These are located at Jones Mill in Hot Springs County and Gum Springs in Clark County.

Although we do not commonly think of them as minerals, sand and gravel are mined in Arkansas. Deposits of these minerals are widely scattered across fifty counties in the state (Figure 45). Sand and gravel account for the largest value of mineral production in thirty-one counties and rank second in eighteen other counties. The leading counties of production are Miller, Pulaski, Crawford, Cross, and Calhoun. One large source of sand comes from the river beds and flood plains of the Arkansas, Red, Ouachita, Saline, and White Rivers. Sand and gravel are washed down into the river valleys and deposited in the river beds. These minerals are used in many ways including concrete highways and buildings. Concrete blocks are used in the construction of houses and other structures. Arkansas has many millions of tons of these minerals which will last for a long time.

Other minerals are found in Arkansas such as barite (used in the manufacturing of paint), diamonds, bromide, and zinc, but only a few of them are mined today (Figure 46). Barite production continues today in Arkansas. Currently Arkansas is second in the nation in production of this mineral.

Arkansas has the only diamond mine in the United States. It is located near Murfreesboro. Although there is little commercial mining of diamonds currently, individuals may come here and mine for these precious stones. A state park has been built at the site.

Mining activities are very important to our economy. Many of the things which we use each day come from minerals taken from

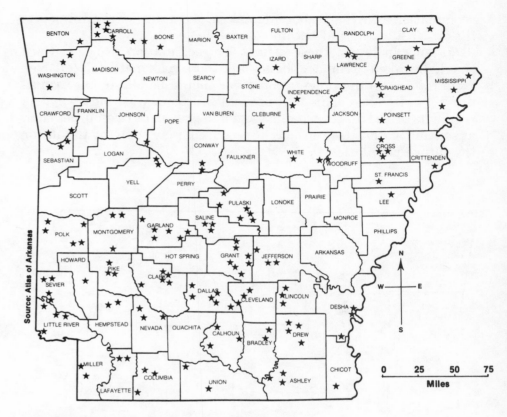

Figure 45. Sand and gravel deposits.

the earth. Mining activities can also be harmful to the physical landscape unless care is taken to protect the environment. Mining can pollute the water and cause erosion of the soil. This is where reclamation efforts become very important.

By reclaiming the land surfaces after mining has stopped, we make sure the environment is protected. Here are some examples of what may happen when mining occurs. A loss of vegetation almost always occurs when mining begins. With a loss of vegetation, there is a loss of soil which is now unprotected. Rivers and streams become filled with sediment washed down by water and wind. Scars of past mining operations are left on the landscape also if reclamation efforts are not undertaken. Sometimes the mining pits fill up with water and become unusable.

Man can lessen these effects by reclamation projects. Care should be taken to replace the soil and loose rock materials left over from mining. A new vegetation cover should be planted as soon as mining is finished. This will prevent soil from washing away. As residents of Arkansas, we must learn to protect our resources such as soil and water. If we do not, the resources may not be available for the future population in the state.

Key Words and Activities

Key Words

Open Pit mining	semi-anthracite
Strip mining	bituminous
Shaft or underground mining	lignite
Reclamation of land	

Student Activities

1. What are the three types of mining found in Arkansas?
2. Describe the ways in which these three types are different.
3. Which counties in Arkansas have semi-anthracite and bituminous coal in them?
4. What is Saline and Pulaski counties' most important mineral?
5. Why are there so many sand and gravel deposits in Arkansas? Why aren't there many deposits in eastern Arkansas?

Selected References

Bureau of Mines. *The Mineral Industry of Arkansas.* Washington, D.C.: U. S. Government Printing Office, 1978.

Mineral Resources Maps, *Atlas of Arkansas.* Little Rock: Department of Planning, 1973.

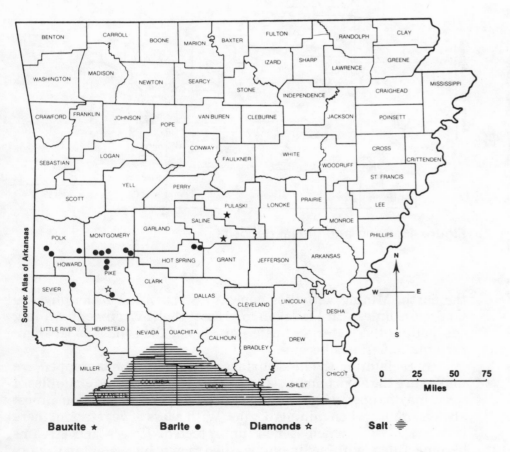

Figure 46. Selected mineral deposits.

Chapter 16

INDUSTRIAL ACTIVITY IN ARKANSAS

Industries are very important to all of us. Many things we use each day come from industrial plants in Arkansas and other states. An **industry** is any activity where a product is made from raw materials or partially finished products. The finished product is then sold to a buyer or consumer. Arkansas' many industries produce a great variety of products. Industrial plants are located all across the state. Why do industries locate where they do? Among the reasons for location are **transportation, labor supply, raw materials, market, power sources**, and the **environment**.

Reasons for Industrial Location

Transportation advantages are very important to industrial location. Because it costs so much to ship raw materials and the finished product, industries try to locate near cheap transportation. For example, industries that use heavy materials like iron ore or coal prefer locations on large rivers or near railroads. In Arkansas many industries have located along the Arkansas River and on the major railroad lines. The interstate highways which link Arkansas with other states also attract industries which use trucks to carry their products to market. Some industries even locate close to airports because they want quick transportation for their people and products.

Labor supply is another factor in the location of industries. Industries often seek a large number of laborers and will located their plant near the workers. The laborers may be unskilled, or they may have special skills needed by an industry. Examples of industries which locate near a large unskilled labor supply are the clothing and shoe industries. Industries also seek a cheap labor supply where they do not have to pay high wages. The absence of labor unions or only weak ones in the area, may attract industries who do not wish to pay high wages.

Some industries require a large amount of **raw material** like iron ore and coal. This forces the industry to locate near the source of materials. By locating near the source, transportation costs are kept low. An excellent example of an industry locating on the site of a raw material is the aluminum industry in Arkansas. The mines, processing, shaping, and packaging plants are all located in Pulaski and Saline Counties.

Industries must sell their products. If a large **market** for the product exists at a particular place, an industry might decide to locate there. In this way, the industry can lower its transportation costs of shipping its finished product to the buyer. Many industries locate in large cities because there are large numbers of buyers. Printing industries and bakeries locate close to their customers in cities.

Most machines which operate in an industrial plant require electricity. Industries which require large amounts of electricity seek out locations near electrical generating plants. Many electrical generating plants locate along rivers where they can use water to drive the turbines. For this reason, some industries locate on rivers close to the **power source**. Many plants have located along the Tennessee River where hydroelectric power is readily available.

Included in the reasons for industries to locate in a state are special incentives such as low taxes, cheap land, and favorable tax breaks. These incentives encourage industries to come to a specific state and often to a specific town. With these incentives, the industries can cut their costs and therefore sell their products at a greater profit.

More recently, industries have begun to locate in places where the weather is mild and outdoor recreation activities are available. **Environmental factors** influence factory location because the employees enjoy the mild climate and recreation activities in their spare time. Arkansas enjoys some special advantages because our winters are mild. People can spend many hours fishing, hunting, and camping in the state's many recreation areas. The environment will continue to be an important factor in industrial location for many years to come.

Industrial Development 1900-1950

Industrial development was slow to emerge in Arkansas. Before 1950, there were only a few industries in the state. In the early years, agriculture was much more important to the economy than industry. In addition to the emphasis upon farming, Arkansas did not have many large markets for products because there were few cities. Among the few industries in the state, the food processing plants, lumber mills, furniture factories, and glass and clay plants were scattered across the state. The lumber and paper mills did sell some lumber and paper products outside of the state.

The food processing industries were concentrated in the largest urban centers of the state before 1950. Little Rock, Fort Smith and Pine Bluff had most of these plants. The lumber industry had over sixty plants in Arkansas and was the biggest industrial category in Little Rock and the towns throughout the Gulf Coastal Plain. Furniture making is an offshoot of the lumber industry. Twenty-eight plants were in Arkansas before 1950 and almost half of these were in either Fort Smith or Little Rock. They located here because of the labor supply and the cities' location on the Arkansas River.

Paper and similar wood product industries were not numerous in the state. Only six plants were scattered across the state prior to 1950. One industry, printing, was found in several cities. More than twenty-three firms in eleven cities existed in 1940. These printing businesses were primarily in the newspaper industry.

Industries in the 1950-1975 period

A sharp increase in the number and variety of industries came during this period. There were two reasons for the change: general increases in industrial production across the United States and the creation of the Arkansas Industrial Development Commission. Arkansas was attractive to industry because of its large, cheap labor supply, low taxes, and tax breaks for industry. The central location of the state in the country plus the availability of major railroads and the Mississippi River network also helped to attract industry to the state.

Little Rock had been one of the few industrial centers before 1955 but suffered greatly between 1955 and 1960. Because of the school integration crisis of 1957, Little Rock did not receive a single new industry during this period. The national attention drawn to the city and the state by the troop occupation of Little Rock Central High School turned away potential industries. Industries saw the city as a trouble spot and avoided it until the 1960's when industries once again began coming to the city.

One of the important changes which came with the new industrial development was the locating of industries in many of Arkansas' small towns. After 1950, plants were located not just in Little Rock, Fort Smith, and Pine Bluff, but also in smaller towns. The small towns had an abundant, cheap labor supply, available land, and low taxes. The towns also provided tax incentives for industry to locate there.

Comparison of Arkansas' industry before and after 1950 illustrates several changes in the industrial patterns. Food processing plants increased in number. The market areas also grew from the previous period. Poultry processing emerged as a big industry, especially in small towns. Food industries preferred small towns because of the availability of a labor supply and nearness to the farm products. Canning companies operating in the Arkansas River Valley and northwest Arkansas began to ship their products outside the state. Among the larger food industries were Tyson Foods, Wilson and Company, and Valley Poultry which located in Springdale and Russellville.

Clothing and shoe manufacturers from out of state came to Arkansas during this period. They sought the female labor supply which was available in small towns. Several clothing industries and shoe plants opened in northeast Arkansas. Most of these had come from St. Louis where they had large factories before 1950. The Brown Shoe and Clayton Shoe plants, located in Leachville and Corning, were two of the firms to come from St. Louis. Important clothing manufacturers included Byrds Manufacturing and Winter, Jack Manufacturing.

The lumber, furniture, and paper products industries also grew in number during this time. Remember that the vast pine forests in the Ouachitas and Gulf Coastal Plain made lumbering one of the state's primary industries before 1950. After 1950, companies like International Paper, Weyerhauser, and Georgia-Pacific built new plants in Pine Bluff, Camden, and Crossett. Location close to the raw materials was the primary reason for this pattern. As the national demand for the paper products increased, new plants had to be built to meet the need. The largest urban areas were the major sites for the furniture factories. The large population helped these industries sell their products.

Metal and machinery industries began to locate in Arkansas after 1950. There were several different types of industries in this group: metals, machinery, fabricated metals, and electrical machinery. Each type had at least two plants in Little Rock and Fort Smith. These firms sought to locate in the larger urban centers to sell their products. A concentration of machinery plants was found in northwest Arkansas around Fayetteville and Springdale. A third concentration of these plants opened in Jonesboro, Blytheville, and Forrest City. They located here since they made farm machinery and wanted to be close to the farmers in eastern Arkansas.

Several industrial concentrations exist today in Arkansas including the central Arkansas area, Fort Smith, Fayetteville-Springdale, the Arkansas River Valley, and Crowley's Ridge. Within the central Arkansas concentration, Little Rock and North Little Rock are important industrial cities. The area is conveniently served by Interstates 30 and 40, the Missouri Pacific Railroad, and the Arkansas River navigation system. Added to these transportation advantages is the large urban population which buys products.

Several urban transportation corridors extend out from Little Rock (Figure 47). Within each of these corridors, many industrial plants are located in small towns. An interstate highway runs through each corridor plus the western corridor has the Arkansas River flowing through it. Most of the towns are less than 10,000 people. **Accessibility**, however, has encouraged industries to locate along these corridors despite the low population numbers.

A new industrial area is developing in Washington and Benton Counties. Centered in Fayetteville-Springdale, this area has a number of food processing and recreational equipment plants. Many out-of-state people have migrated to the area and provide a labor supply. We can expect this area to continue to grow in the future.

Another industrial area exists along Crowley's Ridge in eastern Arkansas. Included in the area are Jonesboro, Wynne, Forrest City, and Helena. These towns are in the heart of the rich Alluvial Plain farming region. The area is served by many railroads and a major state highway. An abundant labor supply and tax incentives exist here to encourage industrial development. Agricultural equipment plants, chemical fertilizer industries, and food processing plants all have located in the Ridge area.

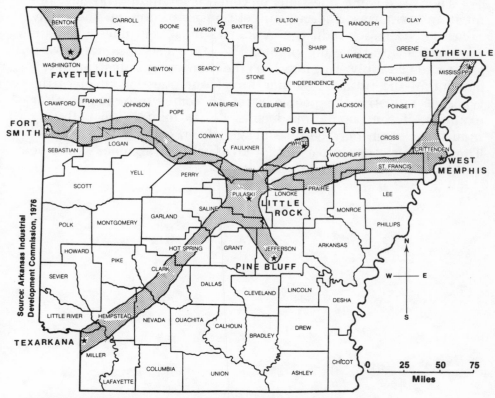

Figure 47. Industrial growth areas for the future.

Conclusions

The future of industry in Arkansas contains both hope and cause for concern. The state's central location in the United States encourages industry to move here. The environment is also an important attraction for industries. Employees will spend more time in recreational activities in the future. With the shorter work week, the nearby rivers, lakes, and mountains will be attractive areas for spending leisure time. Another hopeful factor is the tax incentives. Arkansas' low property taxes and local laws which permit giving tax-free land to industries are strong reasons to locate in the state. These are rarely found in many northern and western states. The abundant labor supply will also continue to attract industries to the state.

There are some questions of concern for industrial development in Arkansas. Fierce competition exists among the many Southern states for industry. Arkansas must continue to remain competitive in attracting plants. The state also does not have a skilled labor supply. This may hurt the chances for industrial development in the future. Another important question involves the types of industry the people want to come to Arkansas. For example, if the population decides not to invite high polluting industries, some may be discouraged from coming to our state. These questions are important for all of us. They are ones which we will have to answer in the next few years.

Key Words and Student Activities

Key Words

Industry	Labor supply
Accessibility	Raw materials
Market	Power sources

Student Activities

1. What are some important factors in determining where an industry locates?
2. What types of industry were found in Arkansas prior to 1940? Where were these located?
3. Name five important types of industry found in Arkansas during the 1940-1960 period.
4. Examine Figure 47 and explain why the industrial concentration areas are clustered around major cities and transportation routes.
5. What sorts of industries are found in your city?

Selected References

Arkansas State Highway Department. *Arkansas Counties: Social and Economic Profile*. Little Rock, 1979.

Arkansas Industrial Development Commission. *An Economic Map of Arkansas*. Little Rock, Arkansas, 1958.

Mapes, Ruth Brown. *The Arkansas Waterway: Peoples, Places, and Events in the Valley, 1817-1971*. Little Rock: University Press, 1972.

Arkansas Industrial Commission. *Directory of Arkansas Industries 1949-Present*. Little Rock, annual.

Chapter 17

OTHER LAND USES

Other land uses include several activities that occupy sizable areas and are crucial to Arkansas' economy. Specific uses include land devoted to tourism and recreation, the preservation of wildlife and vegetation, and lands used to meet local, state, and federal needs.

Tourism is an important activity to Arkansas' economy and the state has set aside sizable acreages of land for recreational purposes. The Arkansas Department of Parks and Tourism has 43 tourist-oriented parcels of land that are either state parks, recreation areas, or historic sites. These lands offer a wide variety of scenic attractions ranging from mountaintop vistas, free flowing streams, shorelines along several large lakes, and numerous man-made facilities such as golf courses, tennis courts, lodges, and camping facilities.

In addition to the state park holdings, Arkansas has two multi-million acre national forests, several state and national wildlife management areas, and 600,000 acres in lakes and rivers. In an attempt to keep pace with the demand for campsites, Arkansas has added over 200 public-owned campgrounds that offer approximately 6,660 individual family campsites.

The rising demand for recreational facilities has resulted from a combination of factors including increased affluence among consumers, increased leisure, increased mobility, and a general feeling of a need to "get away from it all." The average income in the United States almost doubled from $5,601 in 1950 to $9,867 in 1970. Leisure time has also increased from an average of one week paid vacation in 1940 to an average of 2.2 weeks per year. Improved transportation facilities including more automobiles, more municipal and rural highways, and interstate highways have drastically reduced the driving times to recreational areas. These factors plus the desire to break the monotony of a job or get away from the daily routine combine to produce a tremendous demand for tourism.

Government Land Holdings

State Parks

The Arkansas State Parks Division controls more than 42,000 acres of land that it either owns or leases. The 43 separate listings include 31 state parks, 10 historical monuments, and 2 museums. These facilities are widely scattered across the state with slight concentrations in central and western Arkansas (Figure 48) and accommodate a vast number of people. The use at the parks exceeded 6,990,000 visits for 1978, with the greatest usage occurring at Dardanelle where 903,190 visitors stopped at this large multi-purpose reservoir. These figures include both in-state and out-of-state visitors who stop at a park regardless of length of stay. Total use of all tourist-oriented facilities provides an overall economic gain of $1.2 billion for the state of Arkansas. The tourist industry is vital to the economy of the state and represents a major source of revenue. This economic stimulus results not only from direct purchases made by tourists but by an indirect impact as well. Purchases for food, gasoline, souvenirs, lodging, and entertainment all provide an immediate increase in an area's cash flow and indirectly provides jobs for those businesses that service the tourist industry.

The land parcels controlled by Arkansas State Parks range in size from 1.0 acre at Herman Davis Historical Monument in Mississippi County to the 11,644 acres at Hobbs Estate. Hobbs Estate is a newly acquired recreation area in Benton, Carroll, and Madison Counties. The total acreage held by Arkansas State Parks represents less than .12 percent of the total land area of the state. This seemingly insignificant land area is vital to Arkansas' economy and serves the recreational needs of thousands of people. These parks, monuments, and recreational areas generate large revenues and at the same time provide a means by which people can relax, enjoy the

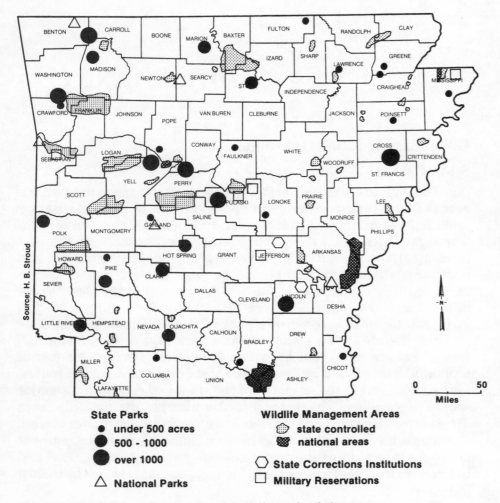

Figure 48. Governmental land holdings in Arkansas.

National Parks

The National Park Service administers five areas within Arkansas: **Hot Springs National Park, Buffalo National River, Pea Ridge National Military Park, Fort Smith National Historic Site,** and **Arkansas Post National Memorial.** The five national parks and historic sites occupy a total of 105,115 acres. More than 95,000 acres are within Buffalo National River (Figure 48).

State Wildlife Management Areas

State Game and Fish Commission Wildlife Management Areas are lands set aside to produce and manage as much wildlife as possible in the existing habitat. These areas are found in all parts of the state. There is, however, a definite concentration of large management areas in western Arkansas (Figure 48), especially along the Arkansas River and in conjunction with the flight path of major waterfowl. These management areas preserve a total of 1,585,945 acres in the state with the **White Rock Wildlife Management Area** of Franklin, Madison, Johnson, and Washington counties south of Fayetteville being the largest, containing more than 280,000 acres. This large refuge coincides with a portion of the Ozark National Forest.

National Wildlife Management Areas

The state also has five national wildlife refuges including **Felsenthal, White River, Wapanocca, Big Lake,** and **Holla Bend National Wildlife Refuge.** All these national refuges are in eastern Arkansas, except for Holla Bend, and occupy a total of 204,538 acres (Figure 48). The main objective of the national wildlife refuges in Arkansas is directed toward the preservation of waterfowl and waterfowl habitat whereas the state wildlife management areas are dedicated to the control and management of all wildlife species in Arkansas.

Other Government Properties

Another service activity that uses relatively large tracts of land are the sites for Arkansas' prisons. The largest institution, **Cummins Prison,** located south of Pine Bluff in Lincoln County, has 16,600 acres while **Tucker,** the second largest prison contains 4,500 acres (Figure 48). Tucker is also located in southeast

natural environment, and participate in a variety of recreational activities including hiking, boating, and fishing.

Public uses of land for recreational purposes include not only land devoted to state parks, but also include national parks and forests, state and national wildlife management areas and many other parcels of land devoted to serving the recreational needs of the public.

Arkansas north of Pine Bluff in Jefferson County. Smaller acreages are used by the Arkansas Department of Corrections at its work release centers and at the Woman's Reformatory in Pine Bluff. Cummins and Tucker, the two largest prisons, are both located on productive agricultural land in relatively sparsely populated segments of the state.

In addition to the land uses described above, sizable tracts are within what has been classified as national military reservations. These reservations occupy a total of more than 100,000 acres and range in size from such large reservations as **Fort Chaffee Military Installation** to the relatively small **Little Rock Air Force Base** at Jacksonville, Arkansas. All military installations are depicted on Figure 48, including **Camp Robinson** north of Little Rock, the **Pine Bluff Arsenal**, and **Blytheville Air Force Base**.

Arkansas has many private and state colleges and universities. The University of Arkansas system is by far the largest land user and occupies approximately 28,000 acres on five campuses and within several experiment farms. Arkansas State University, the second largest university in the state, controls more than 800 acres of land in Jonesboro and 350 acres at its campus at Beebe, Arkansas. The University of Central Arkansas at Conway and other smaller institutions of higher education occupy relatively small acreages.

Private Land Holdings

Recreational-Retirement Communities

The private sector has also experienced tremendous increases in the amount of land devoted to recreational purposes. Much of this land is within recreational-retirement land development corporations that are designed especially to tap the large market for recreational-retirement property. Many of these developments are self-contained towns carved out of scenic wilderness and are populated mostly by retirement age urbanites from northern and midwestern states.

The growth of these developments results from several factors. They include greater affluence, more leisure time, and greater mobility and sophisticated marketing promotion schemes by land developers. These factors all stimulated the phenomenal growth in these recreational land developments throughout the United States. These developments, designed to convert rural land into marketable vacation home sites, have increased substantially in recent years and now total more than 16,000 nationwide.

While not among the top ten land development states, Arkansas has surprisingly large acreages under the control of land development corporations. Among the fifty states, it ranks 11th in the total number of recreational land development filings and 12th in the total number of lots recorded with the Department of Housing and Urban Development. Arkansas, in addition to its appeal as a desirable place for recreation, has attracted many people at or near the age of retirement. Arkansas has 12.4 percent of its total population over the age of 65 and ranks second among the 50 states in terms of percentage of elderly residents. A large portion of these people are attracted to the recreation-retirement communities such as **Cherokee Village** located near Hardy, Arkansas.

Cherokee Village has 2,200 permanent residents and has a higher percentage of elderly than any other resort. **Bella Vista,** a recreational-retirement community in Benton County northwest of Fayetteville also has a relatively high percentage of people over the age of 65. Some retirees are attracted to this type of development because of the complete package of facilities and services that are offered. Bella Vista, for example, offers a house and lot or condominium ready for occupancy and complete medical care at their Concordia Medical Facility when the need arises.

In Arkansas, 357 land development subdivisions are on file with the Arkansas Real Estate Commission. These subdivisions occupy a total of 215,501 acres and have created 143,895 lots. The majority of these land developments are quite small. The six projects that stand out as large-scale operations and actually dominate Arkansas' land development activities are: **Bella Vista** north of Fayetteville, **Hot Springs Village** north of Hot Springs, **Horseshoe Bend** west of Hardy, **Cherokee Village** northwest of Hardy, **Fairfield Bay** in north central Arkansas, and **Diamondhead Resort** east of Hot Springs. These six developments occupy a total of approximately 90,000 acres, or 42 percent of the total land controlled by Arkansas developers. The rapid expansion of these developments in recent years adds a major land use to rural states such as Arkansas.

Other Private Holdings

Literally thousands of small parcels of land are devoted to private enterprises that are capitalizing on the demand for recreational facilities and tourist activities. These enterprises include specialty shops in or near tourist-oriented areas, boat docks, private beaches, private campgrounds, amusement parks of all kinds, and an unending list of similar activities. While the exact areal extent and total number of this type of tourist-oriented activity is difficult to measure, it represents an important source of revenue for a large number of people even if it does not utilize extensive tracts of land.

Summary

This chapter has considered a number of public and private land uses ranging from activities designed for a variety of purposes including: (1) providing recreational areas and facilities to satisfy the demands of a large tourist-oriented population, (2) capitalizing on the desire of many to own recreational real estate, and (3) preserving wildlife habitat and forest lands in various parts of Arkansas.

Public lands, such as state parks, national forests, and wildlife management areas are devoted more to the preservation of recreational resources while many of the private ownerships are motivated by the desire to convert potential recreation sites into profit-making enterprises. Many of these private activities are done without regard for or consideration of the natural environment and their activities should be controlled to some degree either through land use planning or by governmental regulations.

Key Words and Student Questions

Key Words

Tourism
State parks
National parks and forests
Wildlife management areas
Recreational-retirement communities

Student Activities

1. Is there a state park located in your home county?
2. Is it of value to the local community and to the state? Why?
3. How many privately owned recreational enterprises are in your home county?
4. How do these affect the economy of your county?

Selected References

Arkansas National Forest Maps, U. S. Department of Agriculture, Forest Service. Hot Springs, Arkansas.

Brochures from Arkansas State Parks, Department of Parks and Tourism. Little Rock, Arkansas.

Brochures from the U. S. Department of the Interior, National Park Service. Hot Springs, Arkansas.

National Wildlife Refuge Brochures, U. S. Department of the Interior, Fish and Wildlife Service. Little Rock, Arkansas.

Stroud, Hubert B. "Recreational Land Development in Arkansas," *Arkansas Business and Economic Review*. Fayetteville, Arkansas, Fall, 1977.

Chapter 18

MAN'S IMPACT ON ARKANSAS' ENVIRONMENT

Man's impact on the enviroment is very widespread and his changes affect all segments of the world in which he lives. As man builds roads, houses, schools, or other types of structures, profound and often irreversible changes occur.

The preparation of construction sites not only disrupts the vegetation and soil, it also changes the way in which water (precipitation) moves through the environment, thereby altering the hydrologic (water) cycle. Converting natural land surfaces (a well-vegetated area for instance) into man-imposed surfaces, such as buildings or parking lots, sets a number of changes in motion. Some of these changes include: (1) surface runoff and soil erosion, (2) little or no water soaking into the surface to replenish ground water supplies, and (3) increases in the possibility of flooding because of the increased amounts of water running off over these man-imposed surfaces that water cannot penetrate.

Man's changes of the earth's surface have been both positive and negative. In most instances, changes in the environment are made to provide better living conditions or desired material goods for man. All too often, development or industrial production progresses without proper planning and without consideration for environmental damages that may result. Environmental change may also produce a number of accidental side effects. Many industries emit large amounts of noxious gases and solid particles into the air. These gases and particles, when emitted from a large number of industrial plants concentrated in one particular location, may produce a serious air pollution problem. Industrial pollution when coupled with pollution from cars and other motor vehicles, smoke from the burning of certain types of waste, and the emission of pollutants from the various home heating units and from other sources combine to produce severe pollution problems for many cities. Because of the widespread emission of pollutants, smog or a large pollution dome is a common feature of most large cities. A pollution dome is often visible over Memphis on a clear day from Interstate 55 in eastern Arkansas near West Memphis. These pollutants are a serious problem for urban dwellers because of: (1) respiratory problems for inhabitants of these cities, (2) defacing and corroding of paint on buildings, (3) the killing of plants, and (4) the creation of an undesirable habitat for man and other animals.

Air pollution, while more severe in large cities, is also a problem in some rural areas, especially in agricultural states such as Arkansas. Pollution from the aerial spraying of insecticides and herbicides is a particular problem. Air pollution may also occur at isolated industrial sites or where communities are using incinerators to dispose of waste products.

Water pollution is also most severe in or near large cities. Some rivers that flow through cities, such as the Cuyahoga in Cleveland, Ohio are so polluted they have actually caught fire. Imagine calling the local fire station to extinguish the river! Major sources of man-induced water pollution include: (1) domestic waste from cities and towns (sewage), (2) waste from industries (organic chemicals and oils), (3) agricultural waste (such as pesticides, fertilizer, and animal waste), (4) mining, and (5) construction activities.

Pollution from agricultural runoff is a particular problem in eastern Arkansas. Surfaces under cultivation are prone to yield high amounts of sediment that combine with fertilizers and pesticides and collect as direct surface runoff to choke streams with mud and silt and contaminate them to the extent that they are no longer suitable for swimming, fishing, or other human uses.

Even though Arkansas is not noted for its large cities, the disposal of human wastes is causing pollution problems in areas such as Little Rock, Pine Bluff, and other cities where raw sewage or improperly treated sewage is released into streams, rivers or lakes.

Pollution from industries and mining do not represent a widespread problem for most of Arkansas. Industrial pollution is most severe in larger cities such as Little Rock and Pine Bluff and mining activities are limited to several widely scattered areas with significant deposits of bauxite, petroleum and clay.

Construction sites are most widespread and produce sediment that runs off in rivers and streams and into lakes. Road construction is a particular problem, especially where road banks are left unprotected. Removing the natural vegetation without protecting the land, especially if slopes are steep, is likely to result in rapid erosion and increased amounts of sediment for rivers and lakes. Sediment reduces the flow of streams and fills reservoirs (lakes). Sedimentation is largely responsible for the rapid aging of lakes. Some will fill completely with sediment in only 50 years or so.

While any kind of construction is likely to cause some environmental pollution, developmental activities associated with the recreation-retirement communities has been quite severe. These developments have done a poor job in preventing erosion from their construction sites, especially roads that often remain unpaved for years. Environmental disruption is so significant from these land developments because of the complete range of services that these projects provide. The developments are creating suburban subdivisions with many of the services and conveniences that one would expect to find in a suburb or in a city.

The continued success and growth of recreational land developments will generate many landscape changes largely in rural areas in Arkansas. These changes are not always beneficial and may even have a negative impact. Some of the most significant problems that have arisen from the operation of these large developments are: (1) the removal of large tracts of land from alternative uses, and (2) an increased demand on existing resources, including over-taxing public services, such as police and fire protection, roads, schools, and hospitals. These problems are all in addition to the accelerated rates of erosion caused by the disruption of land surfaces for the construction of roads, houses, water and sewer lines, lakes, golf courses, and many other man-made facilities.

As you can see from the previous discussion, man's impact has been most widespread and significant to the geography of Arkansas. These changes may alter the way in which portions of the hydrologic cycle operate, thereby altering the movements of water and the amounts of water available in streams or for ground water recharge. Man may also pollute the environment through careless exploitation in his attempts to convert more and more material goods to meet the ever-increasing demands of our affluent society.

Man has also created numerous changes with definite positive outcomes. These include the building of highways to aid in the movement of traffic, hospitals to supply medical needs, dams to prevent flooding and supply water, contour farming practices that prevent soil erosion and many other beneficial activities too numerous to mention.

It is only when the man-made changes are completed without forethought and regard to the harmful effects on the environment that we suggest laws and controls to assist local and state officials in their attempts to preserve our environment.

INDEX

BENTON CARROLL BOONE MARION BAXTER FULTON RANDOLPH CLAY

WASHINGTON MADISON NEWTON SEARCY IZARD SHARP LAWRENCE GREENE

STONE INDEPENDENCE CRAIGHEAD MISSISSIPPI

CRAWFORD FRANKLIN JOHNSON VAN BUREN CLEBURNE JACKSON POINSETT

POPE

SEBASTIAN LOGAN CONWAY WHITE CROSS

FAULKNER WOODRUFF CRITTENDEN

YELL PERRY ST. FRANCIS

SCOTT PULASKI LONOKE PRAIRIE LEE

SALINE MONROE

POLK MONTGOMERY GARLAND PHILLIPS

HOT SPRING GRANT JEFFERSON ARKANSAS

HOWARD

PIKE

SEVIER CLARK

DALLAS CLEVELAND LINCOLN DESHA

LITTLE RIVER HEMPSTEAD NEVADA OUACHITA CALHOUN DREW

MILLER BRADLEY

COLUMBIA UNION ASHLEY CHICOT

LAFAYETTE